This book is dedicated to my wife—the best teacher I know.

TEACHING WITH YOUR HIGHER POWER

HOW SPIRITUALITY CAN IMPROVE YOUR CLASSROOM

BY
KENNY JAMES

Publisher: Kenny James, M.S., L.P.C., P.C., Ltd
             118 North Oak, Ponca City, Oklahoma 74601   USA
             580.304.9991   kennyjameslpc.com

ISBN: 978-1-7356382-1-8 (eBook)
ISBN: 978-1-7356382-2-5 (Paperback)

ACKNOWLEDGEMENTS

There are several people to thank for their help in getting this book published and distributed. Of course, Diane Szulecki's professional editing and proofreading skills were essential. Thanks also to Derek Murphy, who not only designed the book cover but also saved me a ton of money with his advice on self-publishing.

My ten Launch Team members surpassed all expectations! Thanks, team—you know who you are.

Finally, just a short shout-out to my Higher Power—Hallelujah and thank You!

TABLE OF CONTENTS

Introduction: What Does Spirituality Have To Do With It?.......... 9

PART I: **TRUSTING YOUR HIGHER POWER** . . . **13**

Chapter 1   What Do You Mean By "a Higher Power"?.......... 14

Chapter 2   Teaching With a Higher Power Is Better Than Teaching Without One 32

Chapter 3   To Find My Purpose, I Must Turn My Life Overt to My Higher Power 45

PART II: **CLEANING YOUR OWN HOUSE** **57**

Chapter 4   Will Openly Examine and Confess My Faults to My Higher Power and One Other Person 58

Chapter 5   I Will Submit to All The Changes My Higher Power Wants To Make in My Life 69

Chapter 6   I Will Evaluate All My Relationships, Offering Mercy and Forgiveness to Myself and Others........ 80

PART III: **CONTINUING THE JOURNEY** **91**

Chapter 7   I Will Reserve a Daily Time to Deepen My Relationship With My Higher Power 92

Chapter 8   I Will Remain Yielded to My Higher Power and Share Him With Others..................... 101

PART IV: **CONCLUSION** **113**

Chapter 9   Getting Unstuck 114

Chapter 10   Teaching With Your Higher Power 119

Bibliography 129

INTRODUCTION

WHAT DOES SPIRITUALITY HAVE TO DO WITH IT?

I have been encouraged by others to write this book, but ultimately their encouragement, while necessary, did not sufficiently motivate me to undertake a task I intuitively knew would be both time consuming and difficult. I knew it would be time consuming because I have never written a book before; I knew it would be difficult because, well, I have never written a book before, and I know very little about the entire process. Finally, I hesitated because I was initially unclear about my motive for writing a book in the first place.

In 2009, I began my private practice as a psychotherapist. When my wife asked why I would leave a secure job after 25 years, I answered, "I want to see if I can do it." Writing a book is certainly a challenge, but the thought of doing so "just to see if I can" was—again—not enough motivation for the task.

But I did find the motivation to write this book. Why did I write it? I have an important message that I want readers to understand, I've had experiences that led me to believe in the message of this book, and I believe there is a need for every person (especially teachers) to connect with a Higher Power. Doubtless, many professional teachers do an excellent job of teaching without attending to spiritual matters in their daily lives. However, I believe individuals who regularly make themselves available to a Higher Power can and do improve themselves, their teaching, and the lives of their students.

Anything of lasting or eternal significance is spiritual. So, I meditated, prayed, and explored my inner motives. I realized that no one would stop me from writing a book if I chose to do so, but I asked for my Higher Power's blessing first. Then I remembered the words of Solomon: "Of the making of many books, there is no end, and much study is a weariness of the flesh." Well, was I supposed to write a book or not? No discernible answer, just prolonged silence. I continued meditating, praying, and waiting. There was no miraculous sign, no earth-shattering coincidences, and no confirmation from any source other than those people in my life who thought I should write a book. I realized that I wanted a power greater than myself to confirm my decision so I could gain the confidence I needed to proceed.

Some of you are way ahead of me because you realize what I initially did not: I had it backward. A Higher Power is under no obligation to bless my book writing efforts any more than He is obligated to cook my breakfast. I could ask for such a blessing. There is nothing wrong with making that request. But during one of those quiet times early in the morning hours when I was again asking for this blessing on my book, a thought occurred to me: "What book?"

I answered myself with another thought: "The one I am thinking about writing." The next thought was the clincher: "I don't see any writing to bless." I am embarrassed to admit it, but I needed to be reminded that writing a book is like so many of our other experiences in life. It must begin with a step of faith.

A Higher Power is not akin to Santa Claus, King Midas, or any earthly creature. Thus, one cannot manipulate, trick, or bribe Him into acting a certain way; He is free to bless our efforts, but not required to do so. I continue to pray for a blessing on this book, but I will accept whatever happens, blessing or not. I have just enough faith to believe that since this Power is Higher than I am, He knows what is best, and I do not.

So, I continue making a concerted and consistent effort to deepen my knowledge of, and relationship with, my Higher Power—and leave the outcome of my writing efforts up to His will. I hope you will be blessed as (or if) you continue reading. I will do my best to explain why I believe staying connected to your Higher Power can improve your life and the lives of the students you teach.

In this book I will:

- Define the concept of a Higher Power
- Lay out a sequence of activities that are necessary for spiritual development

- Explore spiritual principles necessary for, and associated with, each stage of spiritual growth
- Address obstacles to spiritual development and ways to overcome them, and
- Provide a vision of the teacher who teaches with a Higher Power.

I ask you to tolerate a caveat of my writing—I use masculine pronouns when referring to a Higher Power. While this Power may or may not have any specific gender, certainly He, She, or It is wise enough to understand that for easier reading, using a consistent pronoun is preferable.

PART I

TRUSTING YOUR HIGHER POWER

CHAPTER 1

WHAT DO YOU MEAN BY "A HIGHER POWER"?

The phrase "a Higher Power" is most often associated with Alcoholics Anonymous (AA), an organization founded in 1935 to help alcoholics stop drinking using a 12-step process. The goal of the process is to achieve a "spiritual awakening" and a desire to practice the 12 steps in all of one's affairs. In other words, those who "work the 12-step program" will ideally realize that this new spiritual way of living is worthy of daily practice in all areas of their lives.

Since this book borrows its foundation from the 12 steps of AA, it is important to know what those 12 steps are:

1. I admitted that I was powerless over alcohol and that my life was unmanageable.
2. Came to believe that a Power greater than myself could restore me to sanity.
3. Decided to turn my life and my will over to the care of God as I understand Him.

CHAPTER 1: WHAT DO YOU MEAN BY "A HIGHER POWER"?

4. Made a searching and fearless moral inventory of myself.
5. Admitted to myself, God, and one other person the exact nature of my wrongs.
6. Became entirely ready for God to remove all these defects of character.
7. I humbly asked God to remove all these defects of character.
8. I made a list of all persons I had harmed and became willing to make amends to them all.
9. Made direct amends to those people as much as possible except when doing so would injure them or someone else.
10. I continued to take personal inventory and when wrong promptly admitted it.
11. I sought through prayer and meditation to improve my conscious contact with God, praying only for the knowledge of His will for my life and the power to carry it out.
12. Having had a spiritual awakening because of these steps, I try to carry this message to others and practice these principles in all my affairs.

These 12 steps have since been modified for use in many different self-help groups, such as Narcotics Anonymous, Cocaine Anonymous, and Overeaters Anonymous.

Although the only requirement for attending an AA meeting is an honest desire to stop drinking, those who continue to attend are encouraged to acknowledge Step 1—that they are powerless over alcohol and that their lives have become unmanageable. According to the late Father Joseph Martin, a Catholic priest and staunch supporter of AA, "That is a terrible thing to ask any human being to do." Why, then, is it the first step?

The answer is twofold. First, no one would undertake a way of daily living that prohibited the use of alcohol unless he was willing to acknowledge that continuing to drink would have such dire consequences that it would no longer be worth it. It is true that most people, alcoholic or otherwise, do not voluntarily seek help on their own. Rather, they are motivated by the consequences of their behavior. It is usually after the alcoholic has lost his job, his spouse, his family, or his health that he may come to this point of absolute desperation.

Second, a person attending an AA meeting for the first time would likely admit that he had tried several times on his own to quit drinking and been unable to do so. AA espouses the disease model of addiction, which postulates that the only cure for addiction to alcohol is complete and total abstinence. According to this model, a person who remains abstinent for several years is still at risk of returning to where he left off if he ever drinks again. Thus, addiction is seen as a lifetime affliction that lasts until death and gets worse (progresses) until death unless it is treated. Untreated, the disease must end in one of three ways: incarceration, hospitalization, or death.

When the alcoholic eventually admits that he is unable to quit drinking on his own and he has been "beaten" by alcohol enough times that he also honestly admits that he has been (and will continue to be) defeated, and that his willpower is insufficient to overcome the addiction, then he may be willing to acknowledge his powerlessness. Father Martin stated: "It is the depth and sincerity with which the alcoholic accepts his condition of powerlessness over alcohol that determines the commitment he will have to the remaining 11 steps of the Program."

It is only after the alcoholic accepts his powerlessness to control his drinking that he will begin to look for an answer "outside of himself." Therefore, Step 2 must come after Step 1, because powerlessness must precede belief in any Power. This seems logical. Why would a person go to a doctor unless he first admitted the possibility of being ill? Additionally, he would do so only after trying all the remedies available to him.

In his revision of the 12 steps of AA, John Baker founded Celebrate Recovery (CR) in 1991. Based on eight biblical principles from a portion of Christ's Sermon on the Mount (known as the Beatitudes), CR, unlike AA, maintains that Jesus Christ is the only true Higher Power. Proponents of CR contend that since "all have sinned, we all need recovery and healing." The eight principles of CR are to:

1. Realize I am not God and that I am powerless to control my tendency to do the wrong thing.
2. Earnestly believe that God exists, that I matter to Him, and that He has the power to help me.
3. Consciously chose to commit all my life and will to Christ's care and control.
4. Openly examine and confess my faults to myself, my God, and to someone I trust.

5. Voluntarily submit to every change God wants to make in my life and humbly ask Him to remove my character defects.
6. Evaluate all my relationships. Offer forgiveness to those who have hurt me and make amends for harm I have done to others except when to do so would harm them or others.
7. Reserve a daily time with God for self-examination, Bible reading, and prayer to know God and His will for my life and to gain the power to follow His will.
8. Yield myself to God to be used to bring this Good News to others both by my example and by my words.

Alternatives to this Christ-centered model of recovery from addiction, hurts, habits, and hang-ups are numerous. SMART Recovery, for instance, uses a nonspiritual, nonreligious approach to empower people to successfully recover from addiction. Secular Organizations for Sobriety is a nonprofit network of secular recovery programs. LifeRing is a secular group that focuses on abstinence from drugs and alcohol. Moderation Management is a secular program that focuses on the controlled use of alcohol in recovering individuals. Women for Sobriety is another nonprofit secular organization for women in recovery.

Spirituality versus Religion

The major difference between spirituality and religion is that religion concentrates on faith in a supreme being, whereas spirituality is more about the belief that there is a higher part of the self and that divine experiences emanate from everyone. Spirituality does not assume that there is a supreme being that dictates how individuals should behave, but recognizes that there is more to existence than the physical world—and that individuals are free to interpret what drives them without being hindered by the doctrines of one specific religion. Thus, the notion of spirituality allows people the autonomy to interpret the spirit or soul for themselves, whereas religion involves participation in a communal practice of divine worship and a specific interpretation of a Higher Power. Religion incorporates aspects of spirituality, whereas those who practice a form of spirituality tend to dissociate their beliefs from the major tenets associated with religions.

It is not my intent to support or advocate for any specific religion in this book. Rather, my definition of a Higher Power is similar to that postulated in the fourth edition of AA's "Big Book":

> Much to our relief, we discovered we did not need to consider another's conception of God. Our conception, however inadequate, was sufficient to make the approach and to effect a contact with Him. As soon as we admitted the possible existence of a Creative Intelligence, a Spirit of the Universe underlying the totality of things, we began to be possessed of a new sense of power and direction, provided we took other simple steps.

All that is necessary for an alcoholic to start their spiritual journey is the simplest of beliefs in a power greater than themselves. The same is true for everyone else (including teachers). Our human minds have a propensity to take the simple and make it complex. We are instinctively suspicious of anything simple because we equate "simple" with "easy." Nowhere is this more evident than in the areas of spirituality and religion. We are capable of mixing religion and spirituality, and when we do, we contaminate both. Perhaps this is the reason why one of the mottos frequently heard in AA meetings is "Keep it simple."

For several reasons, the importance of staying focused on the spiritual—without mixing in religion—cannot be overstated. First, relying on religious beliefs can hinder spiritual progress. For a person to begin their authentic spiritual voyage, they must come to their belief in a Higher Power from their own experience, not from what some external source has told them. If our belief in a Higher Power results from what we were told rather than from what we have experienced, then our belief is not in what we were told, but rather in the person who told it to us. This may indeed create enough curiosity to motivate us to seek more information about spiritual matters, but it will not sustain us for long. Second, mixing the religious with the spiritual invites debate and quickly detours the individual mind from further spiritual discovery. Those who have been sidetracked from their journey may believe that they must defend their religious convictions in order not to betray their own identity. To spend time and energy defending one's religious beliefs can arrest spiritual development for years. Being preoccupied with any of the following may halt spiritual progress:

- Is there one true religion?
- What if there is no God?

- What about the different theories from other cultures?
- Do I have to believe in the Bible?
- Why is there so much hypocrisy in the Church?
- Where did evil come from?

These questions are unimportant at the outset of one's spiritual pilgrimage. Insistence on having answers to these and other religious questions only serve as obstacles. All that is necessary to begin is an acknowledgment that there may be a "Power greater than myself."

Third, religion is often presented as a packaged set of beliefs. Followers of religion are asked to accept as true tenets that they may not completely agree with, such as "Once saved, always saved," or "Speaking in tongues is the only evidence of being filled with the Spirit," etc. Because they are presented as fundamental to one's religious faith, religious doctrines may discourage people from exploring their spirituality. They can be perceived as restrictive and limiting to those who feel the need for a "freer spirit" that they hope to discover on their own. The Higher Power presented in this book does not restrict a person's spiritual path or have any prerequisites other than a desire to grow spiritually. If that prerequisite is met, then all are equally qualified to begin the quest. This includes those who are atheists or agnostics. In the revised edition of *The Twelve Steps for Everyone...Who Really Wants Them*, author Jerry Hirschfield explains:

Neither do agnostics or atheists have anything to fear. They will not be required to change their beliefs. Many of us when we first came in were agnostic. Others were atheists. After the initial struggle, most agnostics had no problem developing a faith in a Higher Power of their understanding whom they often called God. Many atheists did the same but not all. The Program seems to work for both those who did and those who did not. When agnostics and atheists first come to the Program, they often use an entirely different kind of Higher Power.

For some their Higher Power is, at least initially, the 12-Step Program, the power of the group, a sponsor, or mentor. It truly does not matter. If you are willing to acknowledge that there is a Power greater than yourself, then you have already begun your spiritual journey. I trust that this Higher Power will make Himself clearer to you as you continue to seek Him.

There are three traits that a person needs in order to benefit from AA's 12-step program: **h**onesty, **o**pen-mindedness, and **w**illingness. These three traits are the "H.O.W." of recovery from addiction. I believe they are also necessary for spiritual growth.

Honesty is a deep desire to hear and speak the truth, no matter how unpleasant, stark, or upsetting it may be. Indeed, good mental health is a relentless pursuit of reality, no matter what. Finding honest answers means being willing to question everything. It means refusing to sugarcoat reality or speak less than the whole truth. Honesty requires avoiding half-truths in

CHAPTER 1: WHAT DO YOU MEAN BY "A HIGHER POWER"?

favor of complete and total truth. By definition, any Higher Power must be honest and require honesty as a foundational component of communication. Anything less would render this Power suspect and therefore unworthy of further investigation. The Higher Power must be greater than ourselves and so He must be free from the possibility of any form of dishonesty, deceit, or deception. This Higher Power cannot be deceived or mislead. However, He also cannot be so far removed from our earthly existence that He is unaware of our ability to lie to ourselves. In other words, He must be familiar enough with our human-ness that He recognizes that sometimes we can genuinely believe something false (the world is flat, leeches can cure illnesses, or "I don't need anyone to help me").

Open-mindedness is the willingness to take in new information and consider its truthfulness and value, and then change our minds as a result. It is not just about learning new information; it is also about internalizing a "new" truth that may be the opposite of what we used to believe. It is being open to one's prejudice, blind spots, and irrational beliefs and fears. It is a willingness to consider things we have not thought of before. This open-mindedness should not be confused with naivete or gullibility. We have a brain, and any Higher Power worthy of the title expects us to use it in our spiritual lives—just as we do in all other aspects of our lives. If we are totally honest and appropriately open-minded, we will undoubtedly encounter spiritual truths that conflict with what we previously believed.

Finally, if I am willing, then I have not been coerced, tricked, or manipulated into following my Higher Power. Indeed, He can neither force nor convince me. If He does either, then my freedom to choose has been compromised and I am either unwilling or overwhelmed. If I follow Him because of either of these conditions, then I have not done so willingly. Spiritual growth must always be voluntary.

Like every other student who is learning something new, we will be frustrated and confused. These feelings are an unavoidable part of the learning process. We are frustrated because our old way of doing things will not work now, and we are confused because we continue to believe that it should. We do not yet understand why it will not work. The actual learning requires us to let go of what was true and accept and embrace the new truth that we have discovered. Consequently, we must be willing to change. It is this willingness to examine, test, and then change our beliefs, thoughts, and behavior that is characteristic of a person ready for spiritual growth.

The Force or the Farce

Our world is full of opposites. Light and dark; good and evil; kind and unkind. If we accept the possibility of a Higher Power, then we must consider the possibility that there is a Lower Power. If so, what does this Lower Power look like, and why is it important in spiritual matters? Just as I believe in a Higher Power, so I believe in a Lower Power. This Lower Power exists in direct opposition to the Higher Power. Whatever good qualities you assign to your Higher Power, the Lower Power has the opposite. If your Higher Power is love, then your Lower Power is apathy; If your Higher Power is hope, then this Lower Power is full of hopelessness; If your Higher Power is truth, then the Lower Power is only capable of lies, deceit, and misdirection. If your Higher Power is willing to help you become your best spiritual self, then this Lower Power is interested in sabotaging, delaying, or stopping any interest you might have in spiritual growth.

While this implied spiritual warfare is somewhat mystical, invisible, and difficult to define, it is important to acknowledge. While the Lower Power may have many tactics to halt, impede, or delay one's spiritual development, one such tactic is frequently used: substitution. This Lower Power is familiar enough with humans to recognize our understanding of opposites; he realizes that if he pushes his agenda using opposites, he will be far less likely to accomplish his goal. So, for example, if we see an opportunity to help someone else, He may allow us to think, "I should help." But that thought may be quickly followed by another that says, "Now is not the best time," or, "They may be offended by my offer to help, so I could make things worse." Through subtle substitution, the Lower Power has effectively led the (would-be helpful) individual to doubt, question, and hesitate. It is more likely now that the help will not be offered. Consider the following poem:

> **Let there be wisdom and knowledge**
> Knowledge will be enough, wisdom is confusing
> **I will tell you nothing but the truth**
> That is a lie
> **If you look for Me, you will find Me**

Keep looking, that cannot be Him
You may choose for yourself
You do not need any power other than yourself
You have always been worthy
That is unforgivable
Follow Me
Followers are always in second place, be a leader
I do not mind waiting for you
There is no God

While this book is about connecting with your Higher Power, it is important to be aware of other spiritual forces. Since there are evil spirits in the world, we must be discerning. As an example, consider the training needed to recognize counterfeit money. People who receive this training spend little time examining counterfeit currency. Instead, their training consists of examining authentic currency so often that when they do encounter a counterfeit bill, they quickly recognize it because the difference is so noticeable. In the same way, if our connection with our Higher Power is consistent, frequent, honest, open-minded, and authentic, then we will be better teachers.

In his book *Experiencing God*, Henry Blackaby lists seven spiritual realities of the Christian life. Because Christianity is a popular religion in the United States, I have included these realties here:

1. God is always at work around you.
2. God pursues a continuous love relationship with you that is real and personal.

3. God invites you to become involved in His work.
4. God speaks through the Bible, prayer, the Holy Spirit, circumstances, and the Church to reveal Himself and His purposes.
5. God's invitation for you to work with Him always leads you to a crisis of belief that requires faith and action.
6. You must make major adjustments in your life to join God in what He is doing.
7. You come to know God by experience as you obey Him, and He accomplishes His work through you.

If the first spiritual reality Blackaby suggests is true, then your Higher Power is already at work where you are, and, according to reality #3, He invites you to become involved in His work.

Before we get ahead of ourselves, it is time to define the concept of a Higher Power.

Higher Power Defined

I define a Higher Power as a benevolent force that is omnipotent (all-powerful), omnipresent (always everywhere), and omniscient (all-knowing). He is, by definition, a Higher Power. Thus, He cannot be equal to us. This Higher Power is also:

- **Personal.** He wants an authentic relationship with us.
- **Available.** He is knowable, approachable, and accepts us as we are right now.

- ⊘ **Universal**. He is for all and does not discriminate on any basis.
- ⊘ **Spiritual**. He is pure love, and therefore He is not capable of anything else.
- ⊘ **Eager**. He wants a deeper relationship with anyone who honestly wants one with Him.

Let's consider each of these traits.

Personal: The notion that a Higher Power desires a personal relationship can be overwhelming for some people. I recall reading a "Points to Ponder" in *Reader's Digest* about a woman who had attended Albert Einstein's lecture on the theory of relativity. After he concluded his remarks on the vastness of the universe, she approached him and said, "When I hear you talk about the great expansiveness of space, I just can't believe in a God that would be interested in me." Einstein reportedly replied, "How big is your God?"

Available: If a Higher Power is not available, then He is of little practical value. If He is so high and mighty that I cannot or dare not approach him, then why should I waste my time with Him? An impersonal Higher Power might as well be on Jupiter. I believe in a Higher Power that is always present within me.

Universal: He does not discriminate; He accepts all who come looking for Him. He is safe and will not harm you. There are no prerequisites. He does not care about your religious beliefs. He cares about you. He already knows you inside and out and invites you to get to know Him at your pace and in your own time. He knows your weaknesses, your faults, and your dreams. He will accept what you offer, but make no mistake, He is not interested in a casual, temporary, noncommitted relationship. He wants all of you, but only if you surrender yourself to Him willingly.

Spiritual: He is not bound by time, space, or any other dimension. He does not judge by appearance but by what is in a person's heart. He is invisible but willing to reveal Himself if you choose to seek Him wholeheartedly.

Eager: Just as an expectant mother is eager for the birth of her child, so your Higher Power is eager to walk with you on your spiritual journey. You will find Him interested in the details of your life; You will discover that He is not what you thought He was going to be. He is more complicated than you first thought and more loving than anyone you have ever known.

I am old enough to remember using a Polaroid camera. To use one, as I recall, you aimed the camera at your intended point of interest, looked through the viewfinder to zero in on your target, and pushed a button. After a few seconds, the picture emerged from a slot in the front of the camera. It was black. Someone with more picture taking experience would inevitably tell the novice photographer to "wait a minute." Sure enough, within 60 seconds the picture would "develop." That is to say, the black photograph began to gradually change. At first it was lighter, and then, ever so slowly, blurry images of people or a landscape became visible, and eventually you could see a picture-perfect image as the light interacted with the film and the image became sharper and clearer. So it is with spiritual growth. While we may indeed hit a spiritual growth spurt from time to time, spiritual growth typically does not happen quickly or miraculously. Most often, other people comment on the positive changes they have noticed in you before you even become aware of them.

SPIRITUAL PRINCIPLE—FAITH

Each of the first eight chapters in this book is associated with a spiritual principle. A belief in a Higher Power requires faith. Faith is the gap that exists between what we know and what we can prove. I realize that smoke and steam rise and do not return to the earth in the same form; however, I still believe in the law of gravity. I believe in things that I cannot visibly see or prove: The wind is invisible, but I can feel it and see the effects of its existence.

The acceptance of the existence of a Higher Power can be illustrated by another excerpt from AA's "Big Book":

> And acceptance is the answer to all my problems today. When I am disturbed, it is because I find some person, place, thing, or situation—some fact of my life—unacceptable to me, and I can find no serenity until I accept that person, place, thing, or situation as being exactly the way it is supposed to be at this moment. Nothing, absolutely nothing, happens in God's world by mistake. Until I could accept my alcoholism, I could

not stay sober; unless I accept life completely on life's terms, I cannot be happy. I need to concentrate not so much on what needs to be changed in the world as on what needs to be changed in me and in my attitudes.

Faith is a verb. If you have not read the introduction to this book, take the time to do so now. In the introduction, I share some thoughts about asking my Higher Power to bless this book. I explain why there was no indication that He was going to do so. Faith requires that we start the trip trusting that our Higher Power will join us AFTER we take the first step.

I am sure you know that merely reading this book will not result in any significant spiritual development or any noticeable difference in your classroom. The consistent application of the principles outlined in this book will, however, result in both over time. Your Higher Power does not have to be like mine. You can still benefit from reading this book. You already know H.O.W.

CHAPTER 2

TEACHING WITH A HIGHER POWER IS BETTER THAN TEACHING WITHOUT ONE

There are several reasons why I believe the title of this chapter is true. The first reason should be obvious to anyone who has ever taught in a public, private, or Montessori classroom.

Teaching Is Difficult

Teachers' responsibilities include far more than preparing lesson plans and teaching them. Teachers are also responsible for numerous other tasks that may not have much to do with actually teaching. These include but are not limited to: (1) checking for head lice; (2) lunchroom or recess duty; (3) effectively managing classroom behavior; (4) evaluating each student's progress; (4) conducting parent-teacher conferences;

(5) mediating disputes between students; (6) checking students' nutritional, emotional, and social conditions daily; (7) reporting suspected child abuse; and (8) attending mandatory staff meetings, after-school meetings, professional development meetings, etc.

Classroom teachers need all the power they can get, so of course teaching with a Higher Power is better than teaching without one.

Teaching Is Important

Like it or not, you are influencing the next generation. Teaching is second in importance only to parenting. Most teachers understand this all too well and are drawn (or called) to the profession because they recognize and accept the immense challenge of molding young lives. They understand, perhaps better than most, that their relationships with their students go beyond imparting academic knowledge. Holding students accountable for their behavior and their work, while refusing to accept their excuses, requires a firmness they may not be exposed to anywhere else. The kindness and gentleness of a caring adult can never be underestimated. If you are a professionally trained educator who understands the important balance between love and limits and the necessity of both, then you already know how important you are.

I am reminded of experiments by a psychologist, Solomon Asch, who demonstrated the influence just one person can have in a peer pressure situation. After sending a target student out of the room, he explained to his remaining pupils that he was going to draw three perpendicular lines on the blackboard and that one of them would be noticeably longer than the other two. He instructed the students to lie when he asked them which of the three lines were longer. The target student was then asked to rejoin the class. Mr. Asch began asking random students which of the three lines was longer, being sure to only ask the target student his opinion after several other students had already lied. The results, after a series of trials, were somewhat surprising. When there was no one else who would acknowledge the truth, the target student "went along with the crowd" instead of trusting his own eyes a whopping 75% of the time. However, when just one other student did not lie, the percentage of target students who succumbed to peer pressure dropped to only 25%. If you are that one person who will stand with a child when you need to, the child will count you not only as a teacher but also as a friend.

Teachers require students—who may have never been taught otherwise—to apologize out loud, to say "please," "thank you," and "excuse me." Teaching and modeling these "social graces" is just as important as teaching academic lessons. Students learn that not everyone is like their parents. Sometimes the teacher will not bend the rules, believe excuses, or accept late assignments. Sometimes the teacher allows students to fail...experience the consequences of failing...and then to try again when they are ready.

Teaching Touches the Soul

Teaching is important because it touches a child's soul. Maria Montessori, the Italian educator who revolutionized educational practices in the schools that now bear her name, said it this way:

> This is the master we serve, the child-spirit.... We must help the child to act by himself, will for himself, think for himself. This is the art of the servant of the spirit. An art which can be expressed perfectly in the field of childhood. These qualities of a social being are wonderful to behold and the joy of the teacher is to be able to see the manifestations of the spirit of the child. It is a great privilege since usually, they are hidden, and as they appear the teacher who knew of them by the inspiration of her faith, welcomes them. Here is the child as he should be: The worker who never tires, the calm child, the child who seeks the maximum effort and who tries to help the weak, who knows how to respect others and shows us characteristics which make us know him as the true child.

This "true child" is one whose spirit is free of worry, fear, or the need to please others. The Montessori teacher believes that the spirit within each child will manifest itself when there are no longer any reasons to remain hidden. Thus, Montessori teachers must be disciplined in their spirits so that they always first observe and then follow the child's lead and deliberately refrain from interfering with the child's learning while it is occurring. The Montessori teacher guides their students while also allowing them some "freedom within limits," but a belief in and reverence for the spirit of the child is always paramount.

Your Best Will Not Be Enough

It is not a question of if, but merely of when, the requirements of your profession and your life will become overwhelming. You will have those days, weeks, or months when you are hopelessly out of energy, ideas, and resources. If you have not experienced this yet, you will. Reality will collide with your ability, your strength, and your heartfelt desire, and reality will win. You are not weak or inadequate. The truth is that reality overwhelms us all at times. All you can do is hang on and continue to do your best to keep a stiff upper lip. But in your heart, you know you are not giving your students your best. You will use all of the resources at your disposal to try to weather the storm—family, friends, other teachers, sick leave, yoga, etc.—but you will feel yourself sinking faster and faster toward rock bottom. You will probably sense the bottom before you hit it, and you will fight against it with all you have, but eventually, you will have nothing left with which to fight—and to make matters worse, you will be alone.

Our nation saw the photographs of destruction that occurred from the bombing of the Murrah Building in Oklahoma City on April 19, 1995; I remember the devastation that resulted from the F-5 tornado that struck Moore, Oklahoma on May 3, 1999; and it is likely you remember where you were when you saw the Twin Towers fall on September 11, 2001. These are physical reminders of the overwhelming sense of desperation we all experienced as citizens of the United States. A similar feeling of desperation occurs in our human spirit when we are overwhelmed.

This desperation is usually caused by some combination of events that occur over a short period. Most often, at least one of these events is beyond our control. As an example, consider a teacher whose mother was diagnosed with cancer five months ago. Three months later, the teacher's son was injured in a car accident and required hospital care. To top it off, today her car broke down on the highway. The stresses are more than she can cope with. She will recover, but for quite a long time she has feelings of desperation and loneliness. And her teaching suffers.

It is during these times that a relationship with a Higher Power can sustain you. Someone or Some-thing you can rely on to be there for you when there is no one else. Someone or Some-thing you know to be trustworthy. A Power that has your back—and is strong enough and willing to help you. You do not just need *some* power; you need a Higher Power.

There is no use in assigning blame. Yes, you may have done something that brought you to this low point in your life, but like the teacher in the aforementioned example, it is just as possible that you had very little to do with it. Life has hit you with its tidal waves, one after the other, and now here you sit on the beach, exhausted, soaking wet, and alone. Regardless of the reasons why, the simple truth is that life has humbled you and you have used up all of your power.

Although we may be aware of the presence of our Higher Power at moments like these, we may still be unwilling to follow Him. Grateful that our Higher Power exists, and awed by His timing and His presence, we realize that He has carried us (or will carry us) to a place of safety where He will stay with us until we are stronger and able to make our next decision about our relationship with Him.

Sadly, none of us can escape the cancer of pride that is part of our nature. Too often, once we have recovered from the humbling experiences that brought us into the presence of our Higher Power, we decide we can do what we need to do on our own. So, with a nod of gratitude, we walk away from Him and try to make our changes. The Higher Power is a gentleman and allows us to pursue our path, always. He hopes to meet us again—in the same place of humility.

For centuries, psychologists have studied the process of making permanent changes in human behavior. I studied it myself in college and then taught it to others at colleges and universities. What follows is the short version of the "self-help" change process.

Time for a Change

Changing human behavior is extremely easy and almost instantaneous once a person decides to change. However, getting to the point of making that decision—and then sustaining the behavior change afterward—prove to be exceedingly difficult for most of us.

I quit smoking countless times before I decided to quit for good. It took me 32 years to get to the point where I was ready to do it. That was 12 and a half years ago. So, I maintained a daily destructive behavior for more years than not. If I do not smoke for another 20 years, I will be even; I will also be 82 years old.

To change human behavior, four ingredients are necessary:

1. **Motivation:** Like other animals, humans do nothing without a reason. All behavior is purposeful. It is performed to accomplish a goal. I will continue to sit in my recliner forever unless or until I am motivated to do something else (go to the bathroom, eat, mow the grass, etc.). Therefore, the first law of motion is confirmed: A body at rest will remain at rest unless acted on by another force. While the motivation to change is necessary, it is not sufficient to create lasting change. I only need to remember my last New Year's resolution to lose weight for proof that my willpower and determination fade in less than 60 days when I solely rely on motivation to change my behavior.

What is the difference between motivation that results in a permanent change (for me, quitting smoking) and motivation that fades quickly (losing weight)? I believe the difference is the amount of desperation that one experiences. When faced with a very personal and deep level of desperation, then, and only then, is there a chance of permanent behavior change. Examples of such desperation might include a near-death experience, a conflict between a deeply held belief and one's behavior (Is God stronger than nicotine?), a diagnosis (such as cirrhosis or cancer), or a deep desire to accomplish a future goal (walking your daughter down the aisle at her wedding). No matter how strong the motivation, other ingredients must also be present.

2. **New Information:** Have you ever pushed an elevator button again, after it had already been pushed? This is an example of insanity: doing the same thing while expecting different results. Everyone does it. Why? There are at least two reasons: (1) It is all we can do in that situation, other than wait, and/or (2) it may be all we know how to do. If repeated, unhelpful patterns of behavior (these are usually described as obsessive thoughts or compulsive behaviors) are attributed to the first reason, it means the behavior results from a lack of patience and the perceived need to do SOMETHING to speed up the process. Individuals in this situation may need help learning to tolerate a greater amount of anxiety over their lack of control of situations or other people.

If, however, the repeated, unhelpful behavior is a consequence of reason number two, then the person who wants to change will be unable to do so until they are willing to hear and accept new information. I believe that almost everyone does the best they can with the information they have at the time. We do not purposely try to fail. Our intentions are good. If we knew how to program the elevator to go faster, and we were motivated to do so, we would do it—instead of just pushing the button again. Albert Einstein explained it this way: you cannot think your way out of a problem using the same thinking that created the problem in the first place. Changing behavior requires new information and the willingness to accept it.

The **H.O.W.** of change that I mentioned in the last chapter is necessary to "change for good," but still inadequate. What else is needed for permanent behavior change if a person is desperate, honest enough to admit their need for new information, and willing to get and use the new information? There are more ingredients—the lack of which almost certainly dooms all efforts to change for good.

3. **Commitment**: Permanent changes in behavior cannot occur without a high level of commitment. Sometimes maintaining changes in behavior will be easy, but at other times it will be extremely difficult. If the stamina and other resources needed to persevere through the toughest of times are absent, our best efforts will not be enough. When we "hit a wall" and struggle to find

a reason to keep at it, our level of commitment will be evident. At these times it is necessary to close all the exits behind and beside us and remain steadfast in moving forward, if for no other reason than we committed to the changes and refuse to settle for less. We are not willing to just go through the motions of changing to accomplish a short-term goal; nor are we subject to the opinions of others. The commitment to change must come from deep within our very soul.

Surely anyone desperate, informed, and committed can make and sustain changes in their behavior. Unfortunately, these qualities are enough to start the race, but they are not enough to finish it. Another ingredient is required.

4. **Accountability**: A person's willingness to be dependent upon or accountable to another individual is necessary for permanent behavior change. While accountability does not have to be lifelong, it is necessary for two reasons.

The first is that humans are very skilled at self-deception. "I can do this on my own." "I just needed someone to help me get started; now I no longer need anyone else to keep going forward." These are lies that we all want to believe. Thus, we revert to the place we were before we first recognized the need for change. Simply put, we have already proven to ourselves that we are incapable of starting to change without the help of others who have new information. Why would we now believe we can sustain this change without the help of others, too? It is due to our pride and our mistaken beliefs that (1) "I will not deceive myself" and (2) "I can continue to be honest without another person to hold me accountable." If either of the above were true, we would have changed on our own, without assistance from others. We need accountability because even after we have begun to make positive changes, we are still able to deceive ourselves.

The second reason accountability is necessary is because of the human tendency to return to previous behaviors. It is human nature to desire some way of coping with life when we are overwhelmed. It is a fact that life circumstances, in our future, will again be overwhelming. When that happens, we will face a strong temptation to return to former behaviors that will sabotage the new ones we have learned. These former behaviors have worked in the past and do not require the same degree of discipline that our new behaviors do. That is why the percentage of people who return to using nicotine or opiates or to gambling is so high. Without a support system (trusted people) or a reliable individual (sponsor) to help us during overwhelming times, we are highly likely to use behaviors that are the most ingrained and easiest. This is not due to any weakness or lack of information or motivation. It is due to our stubborn refusal to acknowledge this reality: We **still** cannot do it (sustain the behavior change) without relying on a Higher Power. Once we recognize and accept this truth, we no longer resist submitting ourselves to Him and becoming deliberately accountable for our behavior. As the behavior changes become internalized, repeated, and automatic over time, the need for accountability for this behavior change may decrease. By that time, we will probably have identified another area of our lives where permanent change is needed.

SPIRITUAL PRINCIPLE—HOPE

If you are tired of repeating the cycle of desperation–new information–more commitment–accountability, and if you have even a little bit of faith in a benevolent Higher Power, then there is hope. Not false hope, but a real, present hope that has always been available. There is a way to change for good, but it has nothing to do with willpower, self-help groups, or personal strength. He is invisible but personally interested in you and your students. He is both eager and willing to help you as you continue in this profession of teaching and touching the souls of young people. He knows the importance of your profession even better than you do. He has helped other educators, and He can and will help you too.

The Lower Power mentioned in Chapter 1, whom I have dubbed "the Farce," will tell you lies such as "You have failed at your job" or, even worse, "The children you teach have been harmed by your efforts." He intends to discourage you and make sure that you do not follow your Higher Power's leading. Listen to your heart that contains the voice of Truth and believe Him instead.

CHAPTER 3

TO FIND MY PURPOSE, I MUST TURN MY LIFE OVER TO MY HIGHER POWER

Following my Higher Power means willingly putting myself in a position that is behind Him. Not only do I agree to be underneath His authority, but I also agree to go where He leads. Most of us resist being under someone else's authority—it is human nature. I will not be able to submit to His leadership unless I believe the following truths:

1. My way of doing things has not worked out so well.
2. My Higher Power is benevolent and wants what is best for me.
3. My Higher Power is infinitely patient; He will wait until I am ready.
4. My Higher Power will only do for me what I cannot do. I have to do the rest.
5. It is always my choice. He will not choose for me.

6. My way has led to pain and chaos.
7. His way is the best.

When infant children are first learning to walk, their parents know that it is a developmental process. The child will learn to walk when they are ready. It is built inside of them. Parents watch their infant take that first step and inevitably fall. Over and over again the child attempts to master this new challenge. Fall, fall, and again, fall. Parents do not look at each other, shrug their shoulders, and say, "Well, I guess this one is defective, we might as well take him back to the hospital and try to get one that will work correctly!" That's because they know their child will walk. They have faith in the child's ability to learn. They are not discouraged by the child's initial "failures." In the same way, our Higher Power knows our intentions. He is aware of our resistance and hesitation. He understands that we are not good at following, submitting, and letting someone else lead us.

I was both surprised and pleased to learn that Montessori teachers are not called "teachers." They are Montessori guides. This is a subtle yet significant difference. All teachers guide their students. They provide some direction, some corrections, extra encouragement here and there, and perhaps a little more structure for some pupils who need it. Teachers in the public sector must concern themselves with state-mandated educational standards that students must master before they can move to the next grade level. Also, they must prepare their students to take and pass the mandated tests that federal funding requires. Montessori guides, on the other hand, are taught to observe the child closely and then follow the lead of the "child-spirit" as it is revealed. The belief behind this "observe and follow" philosophy is that the child's purpose is within the child, and that purpose will reveal itself to the child if it is guided by someone who has been trained to:

1. Trust the child-spirit to develop when it is ready
2. Respect and value the child-spirit within each student
3. Create an environment that is free from praise and criticism; Guide the child's learning in a way that allows the child-spirit to express itself
4. Refrain from interfering with the development of the child-spirit.

In her book *The Absorbent Mind*, Maria Montessori described three conditions of the children she worked with in India that helped lead to the success of her educational experiment: (1) The students experienced extreme poverty and a social condition of extreme hardship, (2) The parents of the children were illiterate and therefore unable to help their children in learning, and (3) Their teachers were not teachers.

Regarding the first condition of extreme poverty, Montessori wrote, "And as to poverty, it is universally recognized as the first condition for the development of spiritual qualities." The second condition of illiterate parents was "better for the children," because the parents were not able to "help" their children. Montessori believed that most parental help interferes with the development of the child-spirit. She expressed similar concerns about American teachers; concerning the third condition that the teachers were not real teachers, Montessori noted:

> If they had been real teachers, I do not think these results would have been achieved. In America, they never succeeded so well because they looked for the best teachers. Who is believed to be a good teacher? It means usually one who has studied all of the things which do not help the child. Such teachers are full of prejudices and ideas about the child which are not conducive to giving freedom to the child. As is the case with a 'good nurse' who thinks she must help the child to do everything, so these teachers think they must help the child's mind. It is this teaching, this imposition of the teacher on the child, which hinders him.

It is not my intention to provoke the anger of teachers who are not Montessori guides. Nor do I wish to persuade the reader to favor one educational philosophy over the other. However, I do see some similarities between the concept of a Montessori guide and my concept of a Higher Power. In both cases:

- (Spiritual) poverty is a common condition from which we all begin our journey.
- There is a desire for what is best for the student.
- The Higher Power does not impose His will.
- Freedom is the ultimate gift.
- Since we are all children of a Higher Power, we can only discover our true purpose by following His leadership.

In his best-selling book *The Purpose Driven Life*, Rick Warren begins with this statement: "It's not about you." Although written from a Christian viewpoint, this statement is still consistent with my beliefs about a Higher Power, namely that He has a greater purpose for each of us, and that purpose is something we can discover by submitting our life, our will, and our whole selves to Him. Having been instilled with a "mustard seed" of faith, and having been humbled by life so that we recognize we are not enough, we can begin to realize that His way is best—and so we become willing to follow Him.

The Farce will immediately provide us with reasons why we should not turn our lives over to a Higher Power. Among them is the fear that we will become dependent upon and then enslaved by this Higher Power. This suspicion of some "ulterior motive" from the Higher Power is a lie. The Higher Power is eager for each of us to develop spiritually and be freer, not less free. Other reasons offered by the Farce for resisting this Higher Power include thoughts of being rejected by, or unworthy of, His love, or of having to "be good" and follow a long list of rules to stay within His good graces. Parents do not demand such conditions of their infants; parental love is meant to be unconditional. If love is conditional, then it cannot be called by that name. Another noun must be chosen. The Higher Power is Love. Love is not something that the Higher Power possesses. It is not just one of His character traits. It is all He is; a pure Love, uncontaminated by any hidden motive, deceit, or other factors. He is incapable of doing anything that is not in our best interest. That, of course, includes discipline. We will cover that topic later.

Most people are familiar with the exercise commonly referred to as a "trust fall." In this exercise, one person (the faller) stands in front of another (the catcher) and then falls backward, expecting the catcher to "catch" him and otherwise keep him from falling to the ground. If there is sufficient distance between the two participants, the faller will have no choice but to trust the catcher. Having been in both positions during this exercise, I can attest to the fact that there is a point of no return where the faller surrenders the control of their fall to the catcher. It is this kind of surrender that is necessary to continue growing spiritually. It is not a surrender of our physical fall. It is a surrender of our will. Call it what you wish—our will, pride, ego, stubbornness, or human nature. Whatever you call it, we must surrender it to our Higher Power. Of course, this surrender must be voluntary, freely given with no expectations or requirements attached to it. If we have made a mess of our lives, the Higher Power is not obligated to clean it up for us. To be sure, He will assist us by giving guidance if we humbly ask for it, but otherwise, it will remain our mess.

I first began to get acquainted with this surrendering of my will in 2008 when my then 12-year-old son brought home an essay that had been assigned by his seventh-grade teacher. It read:

> Dear Dad,
> Please quit smoking. It is not healthy for you and sets a bad example for us. It stinks and I hope you quit. I love you. *Is God stronger than nicotine?*

I read it, thanked him for it, and told him I would think about it. And I did. I thought, "God made tobacco, so it can't be that bad." I thought, "God probably enjoys a good cigar now and then." But I kept those thoughts to myself because they did not answer the question that my son had asked. The question that would not go away: Was God stronger than nicotine? I soon became aware of two things I knew for certain: (1) At 12 years old, my son would watch to see if I quit smoking, and that would answer his question no matter what I said, and (2) I honestly did not know how to quit smoking. All of my previous, absolute best attempts had failed miserably. Was I going to teach my 12-year-old that the God I believed in was not stronger than some stimulant drug hidden in a tobacco product? What do I do now?

I found myself smack-dab in the middle of experiencing Blackaby's spiritual reality #5 (see Chapter 1): God's invitation for me to join Him had led me to "a crisis of belief that was now requiring both faith and action." Did I believe God was powerful enough to help me quit smoking cigarettes for good, or did I just say that I believed this? I believed He was powerful enough, but I had no earthly idea of how to proceed. As it turns out, that was a good thing, because the path forward was not earthly—it was spiritual—but I had no spiritual currency with which to attack this problem. I lay awake at night because I was aware that this was not a trivial matter of just "breaking a bad habit." This was the definition of spiritual warfare. I knew my salvation was not at stake, but my credibility as a father was. In stark honesty, I began to pray earnestly, "God, help me."

I knew I needed new information, so I went to visit a friend who was a substance abuse counselor. After reading my son's letter, he asked, "Are you ready to become a non-smoker?" I hesitantly replied, "I guess so." With his guidance, we put a plan together that included several "action steps" leading to a quit date three weeks away. I felt pretty good about the plan, especially since it involved a medication called Chantix that I could take for a week while I continued to smoke. After scheduling our next appointment, I prepared to leave, but my friend said, "One more thing, give me your cigarettes and lighter." I said, "I thought we agreed that the quit day was not for another three weeks." He confirmed the quit date and then repeated his request that I surrender my cigarettes and lighter. When I did, he invited me to "Have a seat." Our session was not yet over. He asked how I was feeling. I said I was surprised, confused, and a little jittery. He wanted to know more about the jittery feeling. I told him I thought it was connected to the fact that I had not been expecting to leave his office without my cigarettes. He then explained his reason for requesting my supply of cigarettes and my lighter: "I did that so you would feel the way you do. The truth is that it does not matter if your quit day was today, tomorrow, or three weeks from now as we have planned. On that day, you will feel just as you do now. Jittery, unsure of yourself, nervous, doubtful." He was right.

What he neglected to tell me was that all of those feelings would intensify and persist for a while. I discovered that on my own. Sometime later, while watching a DVD on addiction by Father Joseph Martin, I heard him say: "At the very beginning of his sobriety, the alcoholic, or any other addict, spends

90% of his waking hours thinking about his drug of choice." I realized then that my experience was not uncommon. The human body rids itself of nicotine within three to four days, but no one told my body that. Persistent, intense cravings were usually more than I could stand, so I spent a lot of time praying. I prayed while I was sitting, standing, walking, driving, and lying awake. Insomnia was frequent. I was restless, seemingly always hungry, and increasingly angry. After a week or so with no nicotine, my wife said she was willing to buy me a carton of cigarettes. She explained, "You were smoking cigarettes when I married you 18 years ago. I have never asked you to quit, but we do not have to keep living like this." I was not the only one in the family who had noticed my increasing anger. I was slamming doors and yelling at the kids. I had not had a cigarette in over a week, and I was not happy. Anger is often the first emotion to return when a person surrenders their chemical of choice. I asked my wife not to buy me any cigarettes but to continue being patient with me. She didn't, and she was.

I remembered two pieces of advice that my friend had given me about quitting smoking. The first one was "You do the possible, and let God do the impossible." It sounded like just another slogan from AA, but I resolved to do the possible. The second piece of advice was "Never take the first puff." Solely because of my willingness to surrender my will to my Higher Power, I smoked my last cigarette on April 19, 2008. False modesty aside, this story is more about my Higher Power than it is about me. He sustained me during the greatest cravings. He provided the help, the people, and the resources when I had none. He supplied the strength I did not have but needed to avoid and resist temptation. Consequently, I have discovered through my own experience that He is trustworthy. My son is now 24 years old. Both he and I know for a fact that my Higher Power is stronger than nicotine!

Those of you who are still smoking cigarettes need not fear any condemnation from me. My experience with my Higher Power and nicotine is not about my willpower or determination. It is about His power, which only becomes available when we surrender to Him. I will trust Him to work in your life, as you allow Him to; God knows He has a lot more work to do in mine.

SPIRITUAL PRINCIPLE—TRUST

Perhaps you have heard the story of the man who walked a tightrope across Niagara Falls while a crowd of onlookers watched anxiously. After completing the round trip, he asked the crowd: "Raise your hand if you think I can do it again." Several hands shot up; after all, they had just witnessed him do what he was proposing to do again. He then pulled a wheelbarrow from behind one of the nearby bushes and asked a second question: "How many of you think I can walk back and forth on the tightrope while I am pushing a wheelbarrow?" A few hands slowly went up. Finally, the man asked the most important question of all: "Who's willing to get in the wheelbarrow?"

Trust cannot be half-hearted. To trust your Higher Power requires humility, faith, action, and commitment. Do you trust

Him, or do you just say that you do? He is asking you to join Him, and if Henry Blackaby is correct, when you do, He will lead you to your crisis of belief that will require faith and action on your part. There is no need to fear what lies ahead. Your Higher Power knows what is ahead (He is omniscient), He knows you, and He knows what you need to keep growing spiritually. There is no hurry. He is eternal. And absolutely trustworthy.

PART II

CLEANING YOUR OWN HOUSE

CHAPTER 4

I WILL OPENLY EXAMINE AND CONFESS MY FAULTS TO MY HIGHER POWER AND ONE OTHER PERSON

The next three chapters of this book describe the process of "cleaning your own house." Up to this point in our spiritual growth, we have been led to believe and demonstrated our faith by becoming willing to surrender to our Higher Power. Now, then, we are asked to continue our journey by looking inward, confessing, or sharing our faults with another person and continuing to follow our path forward into a deeper, more intimate relationship with our Higher Power. The focus remains on spiritual development and growth, but now we are truly joining Him as He reveals to us things about ourselves that we either did not know or had pushed down below our awareness. Some people are content to stop their spiritual growth at this point. They may think, for example, "I have quit smoking for good, so I don't need any other improvements now." Others may feel they deserve a break from their spiritual journey and so they stop to rest for a while. While these pauses are allowed, there is more work to be done. And it is important to work. Having come to trust our Higher Power at a deeper level, we are now ready to explore the causes of our problems and no longer content to just treat the symptoms.

Your Higher Power indeed cares about you too much to let you stay the way you are. When you are ready to continue, He will join you. Remember, you are following Him—He is not following you. He will guide you and love you until the end. Dr. Phil McGraw, a popular psychologist of our day, is fond of saying, "You cannot change what you refuse to acknowledge."

Your Higher Power will assist you in becoming more aware of what I call character defects. These are personality traits, behaviors, and beliefs that hold us back from discovering our "truest self." They are defects simply because they hide or obscure who we are. Like thick gray clouds that block the sunlight, these personal flaws keep us from experiencing all that our Higher Power has available for us. A hypocrite is a person who wears a mask (don't we all?), an actor who pretends to be someone they are not. Our relationship with our Higher Power must always be built on a firm foundation of honesty. Anything less than total honesty with an omniscient Power is a complete sham. A Farce. A relationship built on anything other than pure honesty cannot last because it is built on a foundation that contains deceit.

We are all capable of self-deceit. It's not just because we want to cover up our character defects, but also because we cannot always see them ourselves. Cleaning our own house, then, requires another person to hold us accountable. This person, confidant, or best friend is one who: (1) is trustworthy to keep our confidences, (2) is more spiritually mature than we are, (3) is not a relative, and, finally, (4) is not judgmental.

This chapter discusses becoming brave enough to look inward and honest enough to identify our character defects. So we do not pursue this search for personal defects in vain, it will need to be as honest as we can make it (no hypocrisy allowed) and fearless. That is to say, we must be thorough. This chapter also describes the process of being open-minded enough to open up to our accountability partner. Here we become deliberately vulnerable as we share our moral inventory with at least one person we trust. In the next chapter, we will explore the character trait of humility in greater detail. Humility, when experienced often enough, leads to a willingness to continue following our Higher Power. So, let us explore this H.O.W. of our spiritual development more closely. To quote again from Maria Montessori's book *The Absorbent Mind*:

> The real preparation for education is a study of one's self. The training of the teacher who is to help life is something far more than the learning of ideas. It includes the training of character; it is a preparation of the spirit.

I believe that after our Higher Power prepares the teacher, the teacher is then ready to prepare the lesson (or environment). As we study ourselves and complete our moral inventory, we need to keep some things in mind. This exercise is not to be hurried, postponed, or shortened. Therefore, proper preparation is required. While inward introspection is a difficult task, it is not impossible. Our Higher Power is available to help. It is important to contact your accountability partner before you begin the process of writing out your inventory. You may need to contact them if you get stuck or overwhelmed. They will probably want you to call them when you have finished. Once you have requested the assistance of your Higher Power and alerted your accountability partner, you may use any method you choose to write out your inventory.

As a business owner, I am familiar with the need to "take an inventory." If I do not know what resources I currently have, it will be difficult to remain in business for very long. Viewing it another way, this "housecleaning exercise" can be compared to getting ready for a garage sale. You actively search for items throughout your house. You find something of great value that you want to keep. You find some things that you still need, and then you find those items that need to go. Finally, consider an eight-ounce glass containing clear water. Well, it would be clear water if not for the mud at the very bottom of the glass. The mud represents the resentments and other "character defects" that we have toward others, toward our Higher Power, or life in general.

As a psychotherapist, I was asked to work with male juveniles who had committed sexual offenses. As a way of preparing them for the honesty I would require of them, I told them a "therapeutic" story. That is, a story that may not be completely factual but still illustrates an important truth.

Clean the Cup

My grandfather once asked me to clean a glass coffee cup that my grandmother had given him as a gift. She had been deceased for several years, but Grandpa had recently found this glass coffee cup in his basement. It was no longer clear or clean. He told me, "I need you to get this glass cup so clean that both you and I will be willing to drink water from it without any hesitation." He said I could take it home with me, so I did.

It was important to me to please my grandpa, so I spent time trying my best to get it as clean as I could. I used every type of cleaning tool I could find, including Brillo pads, Comet cleanser, Ajax cleaner, and even gasoline. When I had done everything I knew to do, I took the glass back to him for his inspection. I knew it was not clean enough to drink from yet, but I did not know what else to do. My grandpa looked at the cup, then at me. I was nervous, afraid he was not pleased with me. "That's a good start," he said. Then he took his old case pocketknife from his overalls and began to scrape the inside of the glass cup. After a few minutes of scraping, he turned the cup upside down and several pieces of dried-on gunk fell to the ground. "Looks like you have some more work to do," he told me. He assured me that he was not angry and reminded me how important this cup was to him. I promised to keep trying to get the cup clean enough to drink from, and he let me take it home again. He even let me borrow his pocketknife.

I had to work on the cup for several hours over the next few weeks, but I was determined to do my best on this important task. I wanted very badly to see the look of satisfaction on my grandpa's face when he and I could drink from the clean cup. To be sure, I scraped and scraped both the inside and outside of this glass mug. At first, I worried about leaving marks on it, but I quickly realized that there was no way to complete this job by being gentle or by just doing some light scraping. So, I pressed down hard and took my time. When I had finished, there was no gunk anywhere on the glass cup. I tested it by filling it with water and making sure nothing was visible but a clear glass coffee cup containing clear water. I couldn't wait to take it to my grandpa. When I did, he smiled and told me to go fill it up so we could drink. He let me go first. I will never forget the smile on his face when he finished that drink. I knew he was happy to have grandma's glass coffee cup back like it was when she gave it to him.

While working on your written moral inventory, it is important to press hard and scrape your memory, even if it is painful. As far as your Higher Power is concerned, you are a very precious container. Remember the following points as you get started:

- ⊙ There is no right or wrong way to do this inventory.
- ⊙ Do not judge yourself; your Higher Power doesn't, and you are not greater than Him.
- ⊙ He is not surprised by anything you find; He already knew it was there, and He accepts you completely.
- ⊙ Do not be surprised by your emotions; acknowledging and confessing our shortcomings to ourselves and our Higher Power can bring any number of intense feelings, including anger, sadness, regret, shame, and embarrassment. It's OK to feel however you feel; call your accountability partner if you get stuck.

AA's "Big Book" suggests beginning our inventory with a list of people or events that we resent:

> From [resentment] stems all forms of spiritual disease. For we have not been only mentally and physically ill, we have been spiritually sick. When the spiritual malady is overcome, we straighten out mentally and physically.

Using three separate columns labeled (1) Person or Event, (2) Reason or Cause, and (3) How It Has Affected Me, we can begin putting these resentments on paper. By definition, resentment is a feeling of anger that occurs over and over again. Resentments keep us from experiencing the presence of our Higher Power and thus block our spiritual growth. If we are rigorously honest, we will have little trouble starting this first list. I also think it is important to add a fourth column labeled (4) My Positive Qualities. For those of you who have trouble acknowledging your positive personality traits, please remember: "It's not bragging if it's true." You have been given your fair share of good qualities; be fair to yourself by including them in your inventory. I believe if you choose to leave them out, you are insulting your Higher Power and being less than honest with yourself.

There are several worksheets available online and in 12-step workbooks designed to assist with this internal inspection. You can trust that the Light from your Higher Power will illuminate each area of your life that you wish to examine: your fears, your sexual behavior, your business and financial habits, your marriage, or your family of origin. This written inventory does not need to be completed in one sitting. It is enough to start and then to add to it as you think of more to include.

I was drawn to attend a Celebrate Recovery program at my local church. Not long after I began attending their weekly large group meetings, I was invited to join a weekly Step Study. During this two-hour small-group meeting of four or five men, we discussed our written answers to questions in our Participant Journals. For about 14 months, we explored our spiritual paths. That included completing a moral inventory, sharing it with another trusted person, and continuing to practice spiritual discipline, rigorous honesty, and the H.O.W. of connecting with our Higher Power. All of us were initially reluctant to share much of anything, but over time we learned to trust one another and take greater risks. Everyone knew we could stop attending at any time. I was able to complete the first four Participant Journals. When I did my moral inventory, I typed it out on my computer. I divided the narrative report into three sections labeled: (1) The Good, (2) The Bad, and (3) The Ugly. I reported to my weekly group members that I had completed my inventory but was reluctant to share it with another person. I did not see it as necessary. I reasoned that both my Higher Power and I knew of my shortcomings and character flaws; what would be gained by telling another person?

Members of my Celebrate Recovery group tried to explain that sharing my inventory was essentially a test of my humility. Was I so high above, or so far below, the rest of them that I felt I could skip this step? I protested that I did not see myself as either above or below them—I just did not see the necessity of sharing the shameful details of my past with anyone. "I simply cannot see that this is evidence of my pride," I said. When one of my accountability partners asked if I could be deceiving myself, I was a little miffed. He quickly pointed out that there was no need for defensiveness—it was a simple question. I had to admit that I may have a "blind spot" in this area.

I was eventually able to recognize my selfishness and later determined it was rooted in a fear of what someone else may think of me. When I shared this revelation with my Celebrate Recovery group, they smiled knowingly. When I expressed my embarrassment at failing to recognize my selfishness, I was assured that no one thought less of me. That provided the courage I needed to proceed. I contacted a mentor and friend and asked if he would hear my inventory. I began to worry shortly after he replied "Of course." During our time together, we each voiced a prayer, and then I read my typed inventory out loud, waiting for my confidant to interrupt me. He did not. After I had finished reading, I glanced up to find his eyes were closed. He began to pray for me by thanking God for my willingness to share my character defects, my moral inventory, and my humility. After asking God to bless me for my honesty, he said "Amen." When our eyes met, he was smiling. He asked, "Was it as bad as you thought it was going to be?" I just gave a one-word answer: "No."

After sharing my inventory with another trusted human being, I quickly realized that a person cannot adequately understand the benefits of doing it until after they have done it. There is a sense of relief that comes from knowing that another person truly knows all about you and they still accept you as you are. I am not sure what I feared might happen, but when it didn't, I was relieved. The guilt and shame of my secrets had been released, and I felt free! Another aftereffect was a "leveling of the playing field." I no longer needed to wear any kind of mask. I was neither above nor below any other human. I had stepped down from my lofty self-built throne and found that I was just like everyone else: full of good, bad, and ugly—and still valued! Humbled by the acceptance from my Higher Power and the compassion of my confidant, I sat in a great big pile of gratitude for a while. Other character defects began to come to mind in fairly rapid succession. Instead of being overwhelmed by this avalanche of personal faults, I took a deep breath and told myself: "I will deal with these later."

SPIRITUAL PRINCIPLE — COURAGE

To be afraid and continue anyway. Confronting one's past in writing and willingly sharing it with another person is difficult, but not impossible. The relief, freedom, and realizations on the other side of this leap of faith make it worthwhile. With a completely "clean" glass, our Higher Power can fill us with His "clearest water," and we are then in a position to reflect that Love to those around us—especially our students.

The foundation of my private practice as a mental health professional is II Timothy 1:7: "God has not given us the spirit of fear, but of power, love, and a sound mind." Like me, you may be afraid of beginning your moral inventory or of sharing it with another person, but that spirit of fear, while real, is not from your benevolent Higher Power.

CHAPTER 5

I WILL SUBMIT TO ALL THE CHANGES MY HIGHER POWER WANTS TO MAKE IN MY LIFE

At first glance, this part of the spiritual path seems like it would be relatively easy. After all, I have already submitted my will to my Higher Power. I needed to do that to find my purpose. I have completed my moral inventory, which was full of my faults and character defects, and I have shared this inventory with my Higher Power and another human being. Is the next step just to keep doing what I am already doing? Unfortunately, it is a little more complicated than that.

In the 12 steps of Alcoholics Anonymous, there is a pattern that repeats several times: First you prepare, then you execute. You take a moral inventory, then you share it. You become willing to have all your character defects removed, then you ask your Higher Power to remove them. You make a list of people you have harmed and then make amends. This pattern is repeated because it works.

Teachers also follow this pattern in their profession. They earn their degree, and then they are allowed to teach. They prepare lesson plans, then they execute them. They assign homework and then they grade it. In our spiritual life, this same pattern exists. Sometimes your Higher Power will indeed "give you more than you can handle" so that you will recognize your need to lean on Him. Usually, this is not the case. More often than not, our Higher Power prepares us for what He knows is in our future. It is our faith in His invisible guiding hand that strengthens and sustains us when we do not understand why something is happening.

In an article entitled "Nurturing the Inner Life: The Spiritual Preparation of the Teacher," Irene Baker, a Montessori educational consultant, shares the following story:

> Once, when I met privately with a new teacher after observing her in the classroom, I reached over and grabbed the pen out of her hand. Then I asked, "How did that feel?"
>
> "Not good," was her response.
>
> After apologizing for startling her, I explained, "It probably doesn't feel good to children either. I noticed today that sometimes you grab materials out of children's hands as they're working. It's a habit many of us adults have."

CHAPTER 5: I WILL SUBMIT TO ALL THE CHANGES MY HIGHER POWER WANTS TO MAKE IN MY LIFE

All of us have character defects that interfere with our effectiveness. When we become aware of them, we can ask our Higher Power to begin the removal process. Perhaps the character defect is impatience. Perhaps it is something else.

In her book *The Secret of Childhood*, Maria Montessori explained the importance of dealing with our character defects. In the chapter "The Preparation of the Teacher," she wrote:

> Teachers, and in general all those concerned with the education of youth, should free themselves from this combination of errors that undermines their position. They should strive to rid themselves of their basic defect of pride and anger, seeing it in its true light. Anger is the principal defect, but it is cloaked by pride, which lends it a certain dignity that can even demand respect.

The concluding paragraph of this chapter says:

> But still we must be humble and root out the prejudices lurking in our hearts. We must not suppress those traits which can help us in our teaching, but we must check those inner attitudes characteristic of adults that can hinder our understanding of a child.

We are now asked to become entirely willing for our Higher Power to remove all of our character defects. Then we ask Him to do so. The words "entirely" and "all" do not leave any wiggle room. We have learned to trust our Higher Power, and we know that He both knows and wants what is best for us. Why the seemingly sudden need to emphasize "entirely" or "all"? The answer is that the process of spiritual growth is a continuous one. Acknowledging and sharing our moral inventories was just the beginning of the spiritual purification that we need. Perhaps the following lesson about a potter and his clay will clarify this purification process.

The Potter and the Clay

In the beginning, the potter's wheel is not even spinning. It remains still while the potter "works the clay." That is, the potter kneads, massages, and squeezes the clay for several minutes. Before the potter can put it on the wheel, the clay must first be pliable and wet enough to be shapeable. Only then will it yield itself to the potter's hands.

When, in the judgment of the potter, the clay has just the right amount of moisture and pliability, it is placed firmly on the wheel. With just the slightest pressure from the potter's foot, the wheel begins to spin very slowly. The clay does nothing on its own. It simply remains in the potter's hands and responds to the pressure of his hands by yielding itself at all times. Likewise, with our Higher Power. He leads, we follow.

As the speed of the potter's wheel increases, so does the activity of his hands. Moving more rapidly now over the clay, he begins to discard some of the excess clay while simultaneously shaping the clay into a recognizable form. He is remarkably patient. He has a mental picture of his finished creation even while he is creating it.

The wheel begins to slow down. The potter keeps his hands on the clay even when the wheel has completely stopped. There has been an interruption in the creative process. The potter has noticed some imperfection in the clay. It does not matter what the imperfection is, only that it is removed. The imperfection has affected the entire creation—whether it was going to be a bowl, a vase, a cup. Once the clay has surrendered its imperfection to the potter, the purification process resumes. The potter will need to completely start over to avoid a crack or other weakness in the finished product. He stops the wheel and begins to knead, massage, and squeeze the clay so he can once again begin the process of shaping it into a usable vessel. With divine patience, the potter will repeat this process of spinning, shaping, stopping, removing, and starting over, as long as it takes to create the defect-free vessel he has in mind.

But we as humans are more than just lifeless, inanimate clay. We have free will; if we want, we can jump off of the potter's wheel any time we choose, even if the wheel is still spinning. So, what about that? What if we get tired of the spinning and shaping and just want to take a break from all this spiritual growth? How will our Higher Power respond?

He will respond as He always has: with love, understanding, and patience. He knows what lies ahead while we take our "break," and He will not impose His will on us—because doing so would ruin our relationship. Our desire to know

Him, to feel His presence, and to trust Him must always be voluntary.

We may choose to stop our spiritual growth for a time. Every spiritual journey involves a "wilderness experience" at some point. Our Higher Power is still available, but He allows us to be tested. During this time of wandering spiritually, we may temporarily feel that we are free from His shaping, but we are not. Remember that He is omniscient and omnipresent. He is aware of where we are and what we are doing. It won't be long before our "independence" leads us to a point of desperation. Since we have been here before, it may not take as long for us to submit to His leadership and follow Him, as it did earlier in our journey. He is ready to resume our spiritual development whenever we are. In the Christian Bible, the prophet Jonah offers a good example of spiritual rebellion. For those unfamiliar with the story, allow me to present a brief synopsis:

> Jonah was a prophet of God, and as such he was aware of his Higher Power. But when God told him to go to the city of Nineveh and preach, Jonah refused—he hated the Ninevites. He ran in the opposite direction and got on a ship. A storm at sea was so severe that the people on board began to fear they would perish. Jonah confessed to them that he was running from God and that the storm was probably related to his rebellion. He asked that they throw him overboard. (I would rather die than obey my God?) Swallowed by a great fish and sitting in his belly for three days and nights, Jonah finally prayed

to his God. God commanded the great fish to vomit Jonah onto dry land. Jonah then became willing to go to Nineveh and carry out the mission his God had originally asked him to do.

While there is more to Jonah's story, this portion of the Old Testament makes it clear that spiritual development is serious stuff. From the viewpoint of your Higher Power, it is the most important. While being swallowed by a great fish seems a little extreme for most of us, Jonah needed to surrender his rebellious spirit that God met head-on. Perhaps your Higher Power loves you so much that He is willing to do whatever it takes to get you to see things His way. I like to believe that if there was a softer, gentler way for God to get Jonah's attention, He would have done things differently. Because your Higher Power can only act out of love, He may have to take extreme measures to get your attention.

Parents and teachers who have to deal with a strong-willed child know that when confrontation is required, they must be up to the task. If it is a battle they must win, then they do what they must. To allow the child to win in such circumstances is to cause the child to lose respect for the adult's strength and authority. The adult's actions may appear punitive, but they are not. They are motivated by love for the child.

If we are committed to our relationship with our Higher Power, we can be sure He will establish and enforce some limits on our "independence," but only for our good. When we are again ready to voluntarily submit to His leadership, we find ourselves back in harmony with Him, and we are more willing to keep following Him.

I once asked my three-year-old daughter to do something for me. She replied, "I don't feel like it." I met this challenge to my parental authority by kneeling to her level, getting within just a few inches of her face, and then, looking hard into her eyes, I told her: "I can change the way you feel!" She decided of her own free will to carry out the task I had asked her to do.

Like the potter, our Higher Power will not settle for substandard vessels. Over time He will create the vessel He wishes. Because He loves the clay, and because He is the potter, He will stop the wheel every time there is an imperfection in our character that must be removed. He will start over as many times as it takes. His vessel will be strong enough to withstand the fire of the kiln.

To be willing is to go forward voluntarily. Since I have free will, I can choose whether I follow my Higher Power or not. I become willing when I believe continuing forward is in my own best interest. If I believe otherwise, I will balk. When I can honestly desire and pray "Not my will, but Thine be done," I have in effect asked that my will become subservient to that of my Higher Power. It is a continuation of the surrender of our wills that we began in Chapter 3; here, the willingness is more profound and at a deeper level. To be *entirely* willing for our Higher Power to remove *all* character defects is to commit to His leadership from now on. To be sure, our self-will does not miraculously vanish, but rather we have asked Him to complete the work in us that He started. If surrendering our will to His (Chapter 3) is agreeing to "date" Him exclusively, then becoming entirely willing to have Him remove all our defects is to stand at the wedding altar and make a lifetime commitment to this Partner. Just as marriage is different than dating, surrendering all of ourselves and allowing Him to remove all of our character defects is not just "more of the same." We have agreed to "live with Him." If we live with Him every day, He will notice that our defects are more pronounced. He will also notice them much quicker. To surrender ourselves entirely to Him is to accept a truth we have already discovered—that His will is not only better than our own, but it is also the best possible path forward. It is a demonstration of our commitment to follow Him wherever He leads. Even if He leads us uphill. Like all other spiritual qualities, our willingness will be tested.

I remember a conversation I once had with a person who was familiar with the intricacies of training horses. He explained the process of teaching a horse to voluntarily enter a horse trailer. At first, of course, the horse is reluctant and will stand at the entrance of the trailer and refuse to move. When the trainer has exhausted his patience and is no longer willing to continue waiting for the horse to change his mind, he leads the horse on a slow, deliberate walk around the trailer and the truck, making sure to return the horse to the entrance of the trailer, where he will again encourage the horse to enter. He told me, "It is often necessary to repeat this process several times before the horse realizes it is in his best interest to do what he originally was unwilling to do." We are more than just horses, for certain. However, stubbornness is a trait that must be surrendered to Him if we are to be the most effective teacher of others.

There is a repetitive cycle of desperation, new information, accountability, and commitment that we will go through, also. Like the horse trainer, our Higher Power will take us through the cycle as many times as necessary until we realize we are making things more difficult than they have to be. When we have repeated this cycle enough times, we will begin to develop humility.

SPIRITUAL PRINCIPLE — HUMILITY

Humility is, and always will be, at the center of spiritual growth. This character quality only develops after the continuous acceptance of a reality that was initially impossible for us to realize: I am not enough by myself to change for good. I must rely on a power greater than myself to begin and sustain any meaningful change in my behavior. This is not an admission of failure or an abdication of our responsibility for self-improvement. It is an acknowledgment that our best efforts to permanently change our behavior require us to remain humble.

Humility is such that if one claims they have it, they prove that they do not. It is not a quality to be acquired; rather, it is an attitude that accepts the truth of one's limitations. This new humility is the soil in which all other seeds of positive changes in life must be firmly planted. If we lose this humbleness of spirit, it becomes impossible to sustain any future spiritual growth. Sometimes humility is the result of being humiliated; sometimes humility comes because life circumstances have brought us to the point where we realize we simply cannot do what needs to be done on our own. Our Higher Power will continue the lifelong process of exposing our character defects so that we can surrender them to Him. At this point in our spiritual journey, we have committed wholeheartedly to Him. We have thus agreed to allow this "housecleaning" of our lives to continue under His direction. He has always been committed to us.

CHAPTER 6

I WILL EVALUATE ALL MY RELATIONSHIPS, OFFERING MERCY AND FORGIVENESS TO MYSELF AND OTHERS

If we were courageous enough to complete our searching, fearless, and thorough moral inventory of ourselves and share it with another person, we took a huge step in cleaning our own house. Now we are asked to examine our social relationships and continue the housecleaning process. We need to address four steps that are necessary to remove even more mud from our clear glass: (1) We must recognize and accept that our Higher Power has forgiven us, (2) We must accept that forgiveness in its entirety, and (3) We must become willing to extend that same forgiveness to those who have hurt us. It is not enough to just become willing to forgive our enemies—we must also (4) speak directly to them, and offer our forgiveness to them in person, if at all possible. There is only one exception to this social housecleaning: If offering forgiveness person-to-person will injure someone, then we are allowed to find another way to make our amends.

Consider, for example, a man who had an affair of which his spouse or his mistress's spouse is unaware. It is likely that the spouses suspected the infidelity on some level, but to now be rigorously honest and approach the woman with whom he had the affair—in order to make amends— would be to open old wounds unnecessarily. We are not allowed to just run roughshod over other people, regardless of the damage we may cause, so that we can complete our amends. Like all other spiritual matters, we must be willing to acknowledge the pain we have suffered as well as the pain we have caused. There is no room for minimizing pain. Whether received or given, intentional or not, it still hurt. Perhaps a definition of forgiveness is a good place to start:

Forgiveness

To forgive someone is to "cancel their debt" completely. You know that you have forgiven someone when you are no longer hurt or angry or otherwise emotional about the debt they owed you. You are not just numbing the pain they caused or denying it. You have gone through the process of (1) acknowledging the pain, (2) experiencing the pain, and over time, when asked to do so, (3) surrendering that pain to your Higher Power, including all the rights you had to get even or be compensated for the pain you endured. Now, when you are reminded of the unjust pain, you can immediately "turn it over" to your Higher Power because you no longer hold it against the person who wronged you.

Such a surrendering of one's right to justice must, I believe, involve the Divine. It is not possible merely through human kindness. As a mental health counselor, I have been privy to the horrors of the sexual abuse of children, domestic abuse, and the pain that substance abuse causes. To ask anyone to forgive such deliberate atrocities seems extremely unfair. There is always a cost that must be paid before forgiveness can be granted. It is the unfairness of an action that necessitates forgiveness in the first place.

Accepting the Forgiveness of our Higher Power

We welcome the forgiveness extended by our Higher Power. We do, however, tend to "excuse" our sins rather quickly... after all, there were "extenuating circumstances," or "it wasn't intentional, so it wasn't as bad." In his essay "On Forgiveness," C.S. Lewis explained two remedies to avoid making excuses for our behavior.

One is to remember that God knows all the real excuses very much better than we do. If there are real "extenuating circumstances," there is no fear that He will overlook them. Often, He must know many excuses that we have never even thought of, and therefore humble souls will, after death, have the delightful surprise of discovering that on certain occasions they sinned much less than they thought. All the real excusing He will do. What we have got to take to Him is the inexcusable bit, the sin. We are only wasting our time talking about all the parts which can (we think) be excused. When you go to a doctor you show him the bit of you that is wrong - say, a broken arm. It would be a mere waste of time to keep on explaining that your legs and throat and eyes are all right. You may be mistaken in thinking so, and anyway, if they are really right, the doctor will know that.

The second remedy is really and truly to believe in the forgiveness of sins. A great deal of our anxiety to make excuses comes from not believing in it, from thinking that God will not take us to Himself again unless He is satisfied that some sort of case can be made out in our favor. But that is not forgiveness at all. Real forgiveness means looking steadily at the sin, the sin that is left over without any excuse, after all allowances have been made, and seeing it in all its horror, dirt, meanness, and malice, and nevertheless being wholly reconciled to the man who has done it.

We Must Give It Away First

Although our sometimes repeated behavior has hurt Him, either because we injured ourselves or someone else He loves, we expect that the forgiveness we ask from Him will be sufficient to completely cancel all the debt we have accumulated and we can magically and immediately be restored to the harmonious relationship with Him that we desire. He, too, desires a restored harmony, but there is a condition we must meet before He can forgive us, at least in the Christian religion. Immediately after teaching his disciples the Lord's Prayer, Jesus says:

> For if ye forgive men their trespasses, your heavenly Father will also forgive you: But if ye forgive not men their trespasses, neither will your Father forgive your trespasses.

In this case, we must offer forgiveness to others before we can be granted it ourselves. Perhaps karma works differently. To be released from the guilt and shame of our past, we must first release others. This lovingly patient Higher Power allows us to hang on to unforgiveness as long as we wish. Some people stubbornly refuse to even consider forgiving another offender and wrap themselves in a cloak of self-pity and resentment. According to AA's "Big Book," those two emotions are "luxuries we cannot afford." Just as surely as bad cholesterol clogs up the arteries, so unforgiveness blocks the flow of the Higher Power. It has been said that harboring resentment is like swallowing a daily dose of cyanide and waiting for the other person to become sick.

We Must Forgive Ourselves

Refusing to forgive ourselves is nothing less than a demonstration of our pride. To quote C.S. Lewis again: "I think that if God forgives us, we must forgive ourselves. Otherwise, it is almost like setting up ourselves as a higher tribunal than Him."

Some people believe that if they forgive themselves, they make it more likely that they will forget their error and repeat it. To them, continually beating themselves up about their past mistakes is their best protection against future bad behavior. The problem is, this attempt at self-help simply does not work. Constantly berating oneself leads to self-loathing—not an acceptance of the Higher Power's forgiveness. Rest assured, the Lower Power, the Farce, is happy to join you in continuing your unproductive assault on yourself.

Forgiving Others

Appeal to your Higher Power by asking Him to help you become willing to forgive others. A frequent slogan in Celebrate Recovery is "God never wastes a hurt." Loving parents discipline their children, but it is not done out of spite or a desire to injure, although the children may not see it that way at first. Rather, it is to motivate a change in behavior or to prepare them for a future event. All athletes train before they compete. Your benevolent Higher Power takes no pleasure in the pain you have suffered; neither does He waste it. It serves a purpose, perhaps to teach you about the abundance of His forgiveness that you are now asked to offer others who have hurt you.

Reexamine your moral inventory lists of people whom you resent as well as those who have hurt you, and add to it if necessary. Another slogan from Celebrate Recovery is "Hurt people hurt people." Seek the ability to see your offenders as people who have also been hurt.

Discuss your lists with your sponsor, trusted confidant, or accountability partner, especially if there is any possibility of harming someone by offering forgiveness. When your lists are complete and you are truly willing to forgive, you are almost ready to act. Being willing to forgive means you are not attached to the outcome. If you sincerely and honestly offer forgiveness, and your offer is refused, so be it. You have given up the right to be angry about it. In making a genuine, heartfelt effort at reconciliation, you have done what you can. That is sufficient to allow your Higher Power to forgive you.

Now comes the hard part. Call, write, or text the people on both lists, if at all possible. Ask if you can meet with them face to face, at their convenience, to tell them something important. Insist on a face-to-face meeting. Pain is personal; you should not treat it lightly. If you have hurt someone else, they need to be able to look you in the eye as you say your piece. If someone has hurt you and is willing to meet with you, you need to offer your forgiveness eyeball to eyeball, person to person.

Of course, there are times when you cannot make amends or offer forgiveness. The person may have died or moved or otherwise be unavailable for a face-to-face encounter. In such cases, I have asked clients to write a detailed letter to the person and, if necessary, to bury or burn the letter, releasing it to the universal Higher Power and trusting that it will reach its destination.

If you are diligent about making amends to those you have offended and offering forgiveness to others, including yourself, your Higher Power will allow you to experience His forgiveness and mercy. He will completely forgive you for all past shame and guilt. Once you have forgiven others, He will enable you to humbly accept His mercy because you have followed the Golden Rule, which asks us to do unto others as we would have them do to us. (Interestingly but not surprisingly, all world religions have some variation of this rule.) His mercy will be abundant and more than sufficient to completely erase the shame and guilt of your entire past.

Having completed your housecleaning, you will experience feelings of joy and peace. Joy because all of your past errors have been forgiven and you are in harmony with your Higher

Power; peace because you have done all you can to correct your relationships with your fellow humans.

This is a good place to remind you that the Farce is opposed to your spiritual growth and will relentlessly attempt to sabotage it. Often, he will send you thoughts that, like all of his tactics, are lies. Recognize and refute them. Sometimes he will use the media or other people in your life to create doubt about your forgiven status. Hold fast to the Truth you have known.

The implications for teachers should be fairly obvious. Our students suffer when our relationship with our Higher Power is blocked by unforgiveness. There are numerous sources of pain in teaching: administrators with burdensome policies and paperwork, co-workers with attitudes, and parents who believe you should play favorites. And then there are the children, all of them. If I were the Lower Power, I would attack the spiritual growth of teachers relentlessly—if I can get them to harbor resentment and unforgiveness, they will be less effective and the battle for the souls of their students will be halfway won.

SPIRITUAL TRUTHS—FORGIVENESS AND MERCY

The cancellation of all debts owed is one definition of forgiveness. It is motivated by mercy. In other words, mercy leads to forgiveness. In our spiritual journey, we are asked to follow or imitate our Higher Power, who, because of His mercy, offers us forgiveness.

We are to be merciful and give up our right to revenge. If our $10 million debt has been canceled by our Higher Power, then surely He will enable us to forgive the $1.48 that other people owe us. Only when we see all of our fellow human beings as "hurt people who hurt people" can we move toward greater intimacy with our Higher Power, who we are coming to know as Love.

PART III
CONTINUING THE JOURNEY

CHAPTER 7

I WILL RESERVE A DAILY TIME TO DEEPEN MY RELATIONSHIP WITH MY HIGHER POWER

If I may continue to use the analogy of a lifelong committed relationship between two lovers to illustrate our relationship with a Higher Power, it is now time to move to the bedroom. We were in our courting days in Chapter 3 when I decided to find my purpose by turning my will over to Him. In Chapter 6, I humbly asked Him to remove all my character defects, no matter what it took. I agreed to a lifetime commitment with Him. Now I am ready to explore this relationship as much as I wish. I will pursue an even more intimate relationship with my Higher Power, but I will do so privately and slowly. I am willing to become even more vulnerable. Vulnerability requires complete safety and trust, and my Higher Power has proven that He is no threat and that He is entirely trustworthy.

If this analogy seems too earthly to involve a Higher Power, I will remind you of the second spiritual reality posed by Henry Blackaby in his book *Experiencing God*: "God pursues a continuous love relationship with you that is both real and personal."

I propose that there are six characteristics of all healthy relationships:

Trust: Keeping your word and other people's confidences; reliability

Respect: To look up to, admire, treat as valuable

Acceptance: To welcome one as they are; not requiring or expecting another to change

Sharing: Everything—work, love, children, money, tears, dreams, feelings, all of oneself

Honesty: Refusing to be dishonest; telling the whole truth as kindly as possible

Being **Y**ourself: No pretense; no censoring oneself; freedom to relax in safety and comfort

The acronym TRASHY is a good way to remember these characteristics. In a healthy relationship, there is an increasing vulnerability as the relationship deepens, and there is honest, frequent communication about important things like feelings, thoughts, dreams, and frustrations. Healthy relationships also require adjusting to expectations, a division of labor that is fair and equitable, and the self-sacrifice that comes from loving someone else deeply.

How much more challenging is the relationship with our Higher Power? Our Partner is omniscient, omnipotent, and omnipresent. He knows our thoughts before we do. He knows where we have been and what we have done before we met Him. He knows things about us that we do not know about ourselves. The relationship is more difficult because we know almost nothing about this Higher Power.

By faith, we have accepted that He exists, cares about us, and is benevolent. We have found Him to be trustworthy and respectful of our will, and He accepts us as we are at this moment. We have come to believe that He has our back and wants only what is best for us. We turned our will over to Him, knowing that He would help us find our purpose. With His help, we have cleaned our own house both personally and socially. We committed by asking Him to remove all of our character defects. We have followed His lead in offering both mercy and forgiveness to others. He is ready to take us to the next level, but only if we are willing.

I have been married to my wife for over 30 years. She was teaching public school when I met her in 1990. She is still teaching public school (this is year 39). When I asked her for her thoughts on this book, her first comment was, "Please don't give teachers something else to do." If you are a career teacher like my wife, then you know that evenings and weekends are the times when you play catch-up. The summer months—you know, the reason you became a teacher in the first place—are now reserved for professional development meetings, staff retreats, and curriculum reviews.

I will not give you something else to do. But I will ask you to answer these two questions honestly: (1) What am I willing to give up, daily, to deepen my relationship with my Higher Power? (2) Can I do so without resenting it or feeling that it is another chore on my to-do list? If the answer to either question is unclear, please stop reading and come back to this section later.

Your Higher Power has little interest in your to-do list. We usually do not have spiritual development on our list of things to get done. He is interested in spending time with us, and yes, He insists that it be quality time. (Your Higher Power cannot give, and is not interested in receiving, any other kind of time). He knows our busy schedules. From His perspective we may be busier than we need to be, but He is patient. As always, whatever we give up (surrender) must be done voluntarily without guilt or coercion.

When we do find the time, He will be waiting. He expects us to be honest, open-minded, and willing. There is no wrong way to spend time with Him as long as we do so with the following three principles in mind (Dr. Alan Wolfelt shared these during a 2009 workshop I was fortunate enough to attend):

- I must be fully present
- I understand that there are no rewards for speed, and
- I must cooperate with the Divine

Here are some considerations for our "quiet time."

Find a good place: Indeed, our Higher Power is always everywhere, and we can reach out to Him anytime, for any reason. Using a consistent place is suggested because we as humans like consistency, and a specific place can become a place where we always spend time with Him.

Find a quiet place: I realize that living with two children in a small apartment, for example, may not afford much quiet time, but if necessary we could sit in a chair facing a corner while the children are sleeping.

Pray or meditate: This takes practice. Our minds don't like quietness. The Farce becomes especially active when he thinks we are going to spend time with our Higher Power. I heard about a seminary professor who, when asked to begin his class with a prayer, was silent for 10 consecutive minutes before beginning to pray. When a student later asked the reason for the long pause, the professor replied, "If you are going to speak to the Creator, you have to get in the right frame of mind."

Listen: While we should not expect an audible voice, there is a voice to be heard, recognized, and listened to. It is the inner voice of truth and wisdom. It is from our "true self." The voice of our Higher Power cannot be forced or manipulated, but be assured that He wants to communicate with us regularly. He delights in us. How eager would you be to hear your child's voice if you had not heard it in a long while? You would recognize it immediately. You would listen without interrupting, and you would want to hear it again soon.

Study: Read books about your Higher Power; memorize the creed; seek to understand Him by learning all you can about Him. Join a group; follow a blog; find an online community of believers.

Worship: Give thanks, sing, pray, donate, serve. It matters little if you worship individually at the lake, or in a small church with others of like faith. Worship is not a duty we owe our Higher Power. It is a gift of love we offer out of gratitude.

Keep a daily journal: Taking a daily inventory of our actions and being willing to admit when we are wrong (on the same day) helps keep our glass clear of any significant "mud build-up."

Creating a template that contains key topics we want to track, such as gratitude lists, prayer requests, character defects, or even just our behavior during the day, will strengthen our relationship with our Higher Power.

Strive for consistency in all the areas listed above. Your Higher Power does not want a casual relationship. He wants all of you. It is possible to find daily time to spend with Him if you avoid the "time stealers"—i.e., television, social media, video games, and other frivolous means we use to entertain and amuse ourselves. As you deepen your relationship with your Higher Power through daily contact, you will begin to notice some benefits, especially if you can keep in mind that you are the follower, not the leader. I will quote again from Irene Baker's article "Nurturing the Inner Life: The Spiritual Preparation of the Teacher," in which she explains how to cultivate peace:

> Establishing daily habits that promote self-awareness and inner harmony gives us greater capacity to nurture peace in our classrooms. Many people spend a few minutes before meals or sleep remembering what they are grateful for. Other possible practices include:

- Spending time in nature (even just walking around your neighborhood, noticing the trees and flowers)
- Journaling
- Yoga, tai chi, chi gong, dance
- Meditation, prayer
- Silently repeating a simple word ("Peace, Peace") or phrase ("May all beings be happy.")
- Walking a labyrinth
- Reading poetry
- Painting or other creative expressions

Cultivating a peaceful inner life is the foundation for observing and interacting with children with calmness and respect. There are mindfulness and awareness exercises, as well as excellent books that can help us learn to respond from our hearts. As teachers, we have so much on our plates. Start with something small and doable, like taking slow, deep breaths for a minute or two. Then appreciate yourself for remembering to nurture your inner spirit. This practice, however brief, can help you to connect with and nurture the light and inner lives of the children.

SPIRITUAL PRINCIPLES—DISCIPLINE AND AWARENESS

Having the discipline to maintain daily contact with your Higher Power is a lofty goal. Being aware of His presence throughout the day, at a stoplight, during a restroom break, or just before bedtime is enough to start. This discipline is a private time between you and your Guide. It's a time to confess, request, express, and digest all that we experienced that day. There are only two goals:

1. We want to deepen our knowledge of our Higher Power and His will for us, and
2. We want to have the strength to carry out that will.

If we can maintain the daily discipline to focus on these two primary goals, we will notice that we have a greater awareness of several important spiritual realities. We will become aware of our character defects quicker than before. We will also be quicker to apologize. Perhaps most importantly, we will have a greater awareness of the Love within our students as we begin to see our Higher Power in them.

I did not intend to give you something else to do every day. I hope that you will begin to see this daily contact with your Higher Power not as a task to be accomplished, but rather as a Guide to be consulted. I am reminded that the Lilliputians in *Gulliver's Travels* concluded that Gulliver's watch (today it would probably be a cell phone) must be a God because he consulted it so frequently. Our Higher Power is available at all times.

CHAPTER 8

I WILL REMAIN YIELDED TO MY HIGHER POWER AND SHARE HIM WITH OTHERS

Our spiritual progress begins with humility. Recognizing that "I am not enough, and I need my Higher Power to lead me" is a great way to begin our daily prayers and meditations, but the busyness of our schedules, the distractions offered by the Lower Power, and the demands of our jobs as teachers make it easy to forget that truth very quickly once we have concluded our "quiet time" for the day. Our Higher Power continues working to develop within us a constant awareness of His presence so that our connection with Him is not confined to a few minutes of our day. Think of a couple who have been married for decades. Though the two lovers may be separated during the day, each attending to their respective tasks, hobbies, jobs, and responsibilities, they are still "bound together" by their love for each other. Throughout the day, their thoughts occasionally and effortlessly drift toward their partner. When something noteworthy occurs, they may quietly think to themselves, "I want to share this with my beloved." So, as we practice the spiritual principles we have learned and continue to yield to Him, more and more of our devotion, our job of teaching, seems easier. And it is—yet the demands on our time and energy have not diminished. So, what is it that has changed?

The answer is: We have changed. That is, over time we have grown spiritually, humbled ourselves, and allowed our Higher Power to guide our thoughts, feelings, and behaviors on a somewhat consistent basis. We have experienced a spiritual awakening. Whether it happened suddenly in an overwhelming emotional event or gradually over time, we find ourselves in a better place. We are now equipped to experience the joy of living. This new joy deserves a closer look.

It is not happiness. We are happy when our boss acknowledges our hard work on a project we finally completed. We are happy when our spouse surprises us with a gift. Joy is different; Joy is deeper than happiness. It is more profound than our sense of satisfaction with our work. Joy is settled contentment with just a pinch of gratitude. It is more permanent and less dependent on external circumstances than happiness. Joy comes from our soul and is evidence of our cooperation with the Divine. An excerpt from AA's *Twelve Steps and Twelve Traditions* may help explain it:

> When a man or woman has a spiritual awakening, the most important meaning of it is that he has now become able to do, feel, and believe that which he could not do before on his unaided strength and resources alone. He has been granted a gift which amounts to a new state of consciousness and being. He has been set on a path which tells him he is really going somewhere, that life is not a dead-end, not something to be endured or mastered. In a very real sense he has been transformed because he has laid hold of a source of strength which, in one way or another, he had hitherto denied himself. He finds himself in possession of a degree of honesty, tolerance, unselfishness, peace of mind, and love of which he had thought himself quite incapable. What he has received is a free gift and yet usually, at least in some small part, he has made himself ready to receive it.

There is another characteristic that marks our spiritual progress. We are gentler with ourselves and with our students and their parents. The truth is, we are a little softer than we used to be, less harsh, slower to take offense or react. This is not a dulling of our emotional sensitivities or slowness of our mental response. We retain our ability to be assertive and confront others, but we do so with a different level of understanding than before. Now we are less judgmental and slower to anger. I believe this new softer side of ourselves is a direct reflection of the gentleness with which our Higher Power has treated us. He has helped us uncover and remove our character defects, and in that process, we begin to realize that we are a work in progress. Once we can accept our flaws and cooperate with our Higher Power so that they are exposed, we can surrender them to Him. When we have done so, we are able and willing to accept the flaws in others.

It is not unusual for others to notice these changes in our attitudes. It is indeed difficult not to notice a change in one's spirit because it is pervasive. It affects all aspects of our life. We are more accepting of others than we used to be. This willingness to accept others as they are is not only a reflection of how our Higher Power has accepted us, but it is also a result of our increasing recognition that we are now on a level playing field. I no longer need to hide aspects of myself from others. I have no secrets from Him. There is greater harmony between us now. I am at peace with my Higher Power, and so I am in greater harmony with others.

It has become easier for us to love others. This love is not sentimental, romantic, or sensual. It's a genuine desire for whatever is in their best interest, a sincere hope for their best self to be realized. We will not force our new "awakening" on anyone, but we will give an honest answer when others ask us about the changes they have noticed. Following our Higher Power's lead and example, we can remain available to those who are interested in connecting with their own Higher Power and offer guidance and support just as we have received it ourselves. There is no pride or self-righteousness in our offer of assistance to others; we are, so to speak, just one beggar showing another where to find food. Nothing more, nothing less.

Two for the Price of One

We have defined our Higher Power as uncontaminated Love. If Jesus was love incarnate, then this may explain why he answered the way he did when he was asked, "Which is the greatest commandment?" Jesus responded to this question from "an expert in the law" by saying: "You should love the Lord your God with all your heart, all your soul and all your mind."

I find it interesting that he did not stop there. The legal expert had asked Jesus to prioritize the single greatest commandment, but Jesus gave him two answers for the price of one: "And the second is like it: 'You shall love your neighbor as yourself.'"

What was the point of Jesus's additional, second commandment? Legal experts are sticklers for detail. This commandment was not an accidental appendage, and surely its importance did not escape the attention of the people hearing it. I believe Jesus wanted his listeners to understand that a person's love for God and their love for others are inextricably linked. I think he was trying to underscore how the love of our Higher Power must effortlessly flow out from us to others. In other words, He does not bring us to a spiritual awakening so that we can just continue to enjoy His abiding presence in our lives, and that is all there is. If we are unwilling to share His love with others, then we have reverted to selfishness, the opposite of love. If we act "unlovingly" toward our fellow human beings, we show evidence of our character defects. Thankfully, His love is more than enough to absorb our faults. Perhaps we will become aware of them on the same day that they occur if we continue with our daily inventory during our time of quietness with Him. He is quite aware of our imperfections and does not condemn us because we are made of clay. His love remains infinite, and there is no danger of "using it all up."

These new attitudes and attributes within us—joy, gentleness, and (His) love—affect the classrooms in which we teach. The harmony among students increases. Maria Montessori described a concept called "normalization," which, according to North American Montessori Center (2008), can be explained as "the process that occurs in the Montessori classroom, where young children (usually with short attention spans) learn to focus and concentrate for sustained periods of time, while deriving self-satisfaction from their work. Normalization occurs when development is proceeding normally." Montessori felt that a child's troublesome behaviors disappeared when they experienced concentration on meaningful activities, and that children in a normalized classroom will display:

- Love of work
- Concentration
- Self-discipline
- Joy

In her book *The Absorbent Mind*, Montessori wrote: "Normalization is the single most important result of our work." This "normalization" results from helping students work through three stages of obedience. According to *The Absorbent Mind*, children at the first level of obedience are just learning to obey, and as with any other behavior that is being newly learned, they are inconsistent. This is the stage where obedience and disobedience exist simultaneously as the will of the child is being strengthened. The youngster at this point is incapable of obeying consistently. The second level of obedience Montessori labeled "Apparent Order," as the child at this stage is capable of being obedient at all times but still requires the presence of the teacher to do so. As children continue being guided through the stimulation and nourishment of their intellect, they can enter the third level of obedience, which is characterized by joyful, consistent obedience. This third level of obedience is described in an article from the Montessori Print Shop Blog, "Normalization: Part One — Discipline":

> Montessori referred to [the normalized child] to describe the characteristics of the Third Level of Obedience, that is, the true nature of childhood. She maintained that children whose needs are met and are able to develop freely will not exhibit typical patterns of childhood behavior including tantrums, crying, or possessiveness. Rather, the normalized child will show a love of work and order, a love of silence and working alone. He will also show tendencies to work well in a group with a sense of community and be able to show profound concentration, independence, and obedience. Furthermore, a child who shows the true nature of childhood is rooted with an attachment to reality. Likewise, he submits to

> the possessive will because he now knows about the world around him. Most importantly, if the "child's true personality is allowed to construct itself normally," we find he is filled with a sense of joy, and only then will we see the child for who he truly is.

This "true personality" of the child is free to emerge when the right conditions are consistently present in the classroom. Similarly, the True Spirit within us has developed over time as we became willing to submit to, and follow, the leadership of our Higher Power. It is no surprise that our "True Spirit" looks just a little tiny bit like His. Granted, the resemblance is far from exact, but it is still noticeable.

In the folklore of the Incan civilization of South America, there is a story about a Savior who would one day return to rescue his people and lead them to a better land. The face of this future Savior was said to resemble one carved into the side of a nearby mountain. A young lad, upon learning of this future Savior, wanted desperately to be the first to recognize him when he appeared. So, he began studying the "face in the mountain" every day and secretly comparing it to those of others in his tribe. He spent hours studying the face, noticing every detail. Several years later, one of his fellow tribesmen pointed to this now much older man and exclaimed for all to hear: "You are the face in the mountain!"

The dailiness of our journey cannot be overemphasized. The phrase "one day at a time" is heard early and often in both AA and Celebrate Recovery. We have said it to ourselves and others so often that we have lessened its impact. Nonetheless, following this mantra is the only way to live spiritually. This discipline to "stay in today" is similar to the concept of mindfulness in the psychological world. To be fully present in the moment requires learning to focus our attention on what is happening now, while paying less attention to thoughts and worries about the future as well as the regrets of the past that the Lower Power, the Farce, will so frequently remind us of.

In his book *How to Stop Worrying and Start Living*, Dale Carnegie describes German submarines called "U-boats" used in the Second World War. They were constructed in a way that allowed both the front and rear portions of the vessel to be sealed off from the rest of the submarine. This meant that enemy torpedoes would have to hit the U-boat more than once to disable it and that the crew aboard the U-boat could continue to survive in the middle portion of the submarine. Carnegie suggests that we learn to "seal off" both yesterday and tomorrow so that we may fully live today.

Pride is a stubborn rascal. Like a conjoined twin, it is always with us. Regardless of our present degree of humility, it will not go away for long. This enemy of spiritual development is a lifetime companion that we must continually be aware of and contend with. Sometimes it seems as if it just came out of nowhere, but we know the truth—it came from inside us. The existence of our ever-present ego is why we must make deliberate efforts to stay yielded to Him and to share His love with those around us. We have come to learn that this yielding of ourselves is not burdensome. We now recognize it as beneficial and best for us. Although we earnestly desire to follow His lead, pride pulls our hearts in the opposite direction. Because we are willing to "keep the faith" and exercise the discipline necessary to maintain daily contact with Him, we are much quicker to recognize when our ego rears its ugly head. We sincerely apologize to others now when we may have injured them. We are no longer content to "just let it slide." It is with immense gratitude and humility that we realize He is leading us to love as He loves.

I will quote again from Montessori's *The Absorbent Mind*. In its closing, she wrote of love:

> Love is a gift of the Universal Consciousness for a special aim and purpose as is everything lent to man by the Cosmic Consciousness. If the aim is not fulfilled, then nothing can sustain itself and all crumbles away. We can understand the words of the saint that all is nothing unless love is there. More than electricity which gives light in the darkness, more than the etheric waves which allow our voices to travel over wide distances, more than any energy that man has discovered and exploited is this love; above all things it is the most important. All that man can do with the forces of electricity or of etheric waves depends on the consciousness of him who uses it. The energy of love is given to us so that each one of us contains it when a child comes and it opens out as a fan. Even if later circumstances destroy it, we feel a yearning for it. So we must study it and use it more than any other force in the environment, because it is not lent to the environment as other forces are, but it

is lent to us. The study of love and its utilization will lead us to the fountain whence it springs and that is the Child. This is the new path that man must follow.

SPIRITUAL PRINCIPLES — LOVE AND SERVICE

Having been the recipient of our Higher Power's love, we desire more of it. The more we are ready and willing to receive, the more we absorb; the more we absorb, the more we imitate Him—the source of this love in the first place. As we imitate Him, others, including our students, are positively affected, even if they don't realize it. This love does not just reveal itself via our hugs and kisses, although they may be freely given, but rather His love is more accurately reflected in our humble acts of service to others.

Our service to others, like the other spiritual principles we have encountered on our journey, does not come from a sense of duty or obligation. It is given voluntarily with no requirement or expectation of return. Our service is an act of worship, offered from our spirit, which now more closely resembles His.

PART IV
CONCLUSION

CHAPTER 9

GETTING UNSTUCK

We will get stuck. Our spiritual development is not linear. There are fits and starts, peaks, plateaus, and valleys. Getting stuck is different than getting off track. That can happen, too. If it does: (1) take note of your current position, (2) create a plan to get back on track, and then (3) implement your plan. Easy enough. But what if you get stuck and you realize you are not moving at all? Or perhaps you realize you haven't moved in quite a while and there is zero momentum. Now what to do?

If you have ever gotten a vehicle stuck, then you probably did what most people do. First, you tried harder, gave it more gas; maybe you even "floored it." The result of trying harder is usually getting more stuck than you were. Next, we might try to help the tires get more traction by throwing some kitty litter or salt under them. When that does not work, we may get out and try to push the vehicle out by rocking it back and forth, hoping to generate enough momentum to get the vehicle out of the hole. If we have concluded that we cannot get unstuck on our own, then we will call for help; if our friends and family are unable to get us unstuck, then we will reluctantly call, and pay for, a professional towing service.

Getting spiritually stuck can feel the same way. We notice that we are bored, and everything starts to look the same. Excitement, contentment, and joy are absent. Blah! We seem to be just going through the motions, and we realize we are in a rut. To begin the process of getting "unstuck," I suggest we examine our "6 pack," as I call it:

1. **Protect your quiet time.** This daily contact with your Higher Power is the source of your strength and purpose. We all get stuck when this time is no longer a top priority in our day.
2. **Examine your schedule.** Keep a log of your activities for a week so you can identify where you are spending your energy.
3. **Review what has worked in the past.** Things may have changed in your life, but your Higher Power has not. What worked in the past may not work now, but it is a good place to begin to figure out what you may need to return to doing.
4. **Reconnect with family, friends, and people of like faith.** Remember that faith is a verb; feeling better usually comes after the doing, not before.
5. **Keep your balance.** All things in moderation; stay busy, but not too busy.
6. **Get help if you need to.** Pride keeps us stuck and makes the Farce happy.

Sometimes we can feel stuck when we are not. An example is when we are dissatisfied with our spiritual progress because we expected our Higher Power to do something He has not done; we might even be angry with Him and pout for a while. This is more common than you might imagine. In such cases, we may be allowed to pout until we get tired of pouting. Our Higher Power is not motivated by our emotional tantrums, even if we feel they are justified. Our Higher Power knows why we are acting the way we are. Perhaps we need to return to the H.O.W. of spiritual progress.

Another common reason for feeling stuck is regression. It's not so much that we have backslidden, it's more like we have reverted to an earlier stage of our development. Children will often regress when they are stressed: A seven-year-old begins to wet the bed a few times a week; a three-year-old starts using baby talk or suddenly becomes extremely clingy to her parents. These are signs that a child's coping skills have been exceeded. If you suspect you may have regressed, review the developmental sequence outlined in this book to determine your "spiritual location" while asking your Higher Power for clarity and direction.

You can perform a kind of "spiritual check-up"—similar to a medical doctor taking your vital signs—by honestly examining your measure of the spiritual principles covered in this book: Faith, Hope, Trust and Surrender, Honesty, Courage, Humility, Mercy and Forgiveness, Discipline and Awareness, Love and Service. If you identify a deficit, ask for your Higher Power's assistance in correcting it.

We can quickly lose our way when we forget our purpose and unintentionally "disconnect" from our Higher Power. I once unplugged our alarm clock when I accidentally ran over the cord with the vacuum cleaner. I did not realize it until the next morning. We don't intend to neglect our spiritual disciplines, but we can fall prey to the schemes of the Farce. He will use any number of tactics to interfere with our relationship with our Higher Power, including substitution, distraction, depression, anxiety, financial difficulties, and marital or family issues. All of these serve to take our focus away from our daily reliance on our Higher Power.

Why Did You Get Stuck?

It is more important to get "unstuck" than it is to figure out why you got stuck in the first place. However, figuring out why you got stuck is important. When I work with people in my counseling business, I provide them six steps to follow after they have "messed up":

1. Admit it out loud to the person whom you have offended.
2. Apologize sincerely, stating exactly what you are sorry for.
3. Ask the question, "What can I do to make it up to you?"
4. Forgive yourself.
5. Learn the lesson (Why did you do what you did?).
6. Don't repeat the behavior.

It's a rather simple process, but it works. The goal is often to repair the damage in the relationship. If we are trying to determine why we got stuck in our spiritual journey, perhaps we have neglected our most important Client. Although our Higher Power understands our daily preoccupations, the old saying is still true: "If you don't feel close to God, guess who moved."

CHAPTER 10

TEACHING WITH YOUR HIGHER POWER

Throughout this book, I have touched upon some of the differences between public schools, private schools, and Montessori schools. In this chapter, I will describe my vision for you as an educator who is committed to your profession, your spiritual growth, and the welfare of the children entrusted to you. We will begin by examining the similarities and differences between teachers who invite their Higher Power into their lives and classrooms and those who do not. Then I will use both a poem and an analogy to point out some differences in the perspectives of those educators who teach with their Higher Power in mind versus those who do not.

I will share my hope and expectation that you will have many awesome days in your spiritual journey and that you will recognize them as a gift from your Higher Power. Finally, I will quote from Maria Montessori's *The Absorbent Mind* one last time.

Similarities Among Teachers

If you stay in the teaching profession for more than a few years, you will meet other professionals who share some common values and experiences with you. For example, almost every educator has a love of children and a strong desire to make a positive difference in the lives of their students. These two qualities may be enough to draw you to the teaching profession, but they will not sustain you long given all the demands placed upon you.

Career teachers have found other resources to sustain themselves, such as mentors and close relationships with fellow teachers, co-workers, administrators, friends, and family members. Perhaps they have supportive spouses or trusted confidants to whom they can safely vent.

They also have experience. They have learned how to manage students with special needs as well as children who come from varying family backgrounds and situations. They are likely to have attended more professional training seminars than anyone else they know. Because of their experience, they know their strengths and weaknesses. These experienced teachers can read students well, sometimes even better than the child's parents. They are no longer intimidated by parent-teacher conferences, professional evaluations, or so-called "experts" in classroom management.

They are committed to their profession and to being the best they can be for the sake of their students. They simply cannot settle for mediocre performance, either in themselves or their students. They are achievement-motivated and results-oriented. Veteran teachers also have resources that they have developed over the years, and they are willing to use all of them to benefit their students.

Differences When Teaching With a Higher Power

I must say to those of you who teach with a Higher Power—whether now or in the future—you are not different from any other teacher in the ways I've mentioned thus far. The differences I note here are differences in your classroom, and in yourself, not in your dedication to your students, your profession, or your abilities. Your Higher Power cannot operate in a classroom led by a pious, self-righteous individual who is secretly proud of their superiority because they claim to be teaching with a Higher Power. Without an abundance of personal genuine humility, there will not be any evidence of a Higher Power at work in your classroom. The Farce has a vast storehouse of "false modesty," and he is willing to give you all that you could want.

Those who teach with a Higher Power have the following characteristics and attitudes:

They are aware of the bigger picture. They not only believe in a Higher Power, but they also have the faith and humility to recognize that He can do what they cannot. They desire to cooperate with the Divine.

They recognize the importance of the child-spirit. They know that their position as a teacher allows them to observe the child-spirit, which they see as eternal.

They prepare themselves spiritually. Teaching with a Higher Power is more than just an awareness that He exists. It is also believing that He is personal and eager to join them in the classroom. Consequently, He becomes a priority in their lives.

They are grateful, humble, joyous, and quick to forgive. They earnestly try to imitate their Higher Power by remaining yielded to His Spirit.

They do not take themselves too seriously. They are not too proud to admit their shortcomings and faux pas. They tend to laugh a lot at themselves.

Their students' happiness is secondary to their normalization. Teachers who teach with a Higher Power are aware of the need to lead each child to their own inner strengths and will not allow the child or other students to interfere with this process.

They take great care to present and maintain an orderly classroom environment. Since disorder invites chaos, and chaos interferes with normalization, they do spend more time (usually during the evening and on weekends) getting things ready ahead of time so that they can attend to their students' needs in an unhurried manner.

They are intentional about their spiritual health and well-being. They are not content just to exercise good self-care and worship regularly. Their spiritual disciplines occur daily and throughout the day. They reflect on spiritual matters frequently and involve others in their spiritual voyage.

Whose Children?

In Kahlil Gibran's *The Prophet*, there is a poem entitled "On Children":

And a woman who held a babe against her bosom said,
Speak to us of Children.
And he said:
Your children are not your children.
They are the sons and daughters of Life's longing for itself.
They come through you but not from you,
And though they are with you yet they belong not to you.

You may give them your love but not your thoughts,
For they have their thoughts.
You may house their bodies but not their souls,
For their souls dwell in the house of tomorrow, which you cannot visit, not even in your dreams.
You may strive to be like them, but seek not to make them like you.
For life goes not backward nor tarries with yesterday.
You are the bows from which your children as living arrows are sent forth.
The archer sees the mark upon the path of the infinite, and He bends you with His might that His arrows may go swift and far.

Let your bending in the archer's hand be for gladness;
For even as He loves the arrow that flies, so He loves also the bow that is stable.

Let us not forget that your students are not yours. You do have a "sacred" responsibility *to* them, but you are not responsible *for* them.

Water Bottles

As I write this chapter, our world is waiting on a vaccine for the coronavirus that has led to a pandemic. For this reason, the current school year will be significantly different for everyone. Students will have to "unlearn" those lessons taught in preschool and kindergarten, which have been replaced by new rules:

- Don't share with others; we can't risk contamination.
- Stay at least six feet apart, especially on the playground.
- Cover your cough, sneeze, or any other droplet that may come from your mouth or nose.
- You cannot hold hands with other students.
- Only drink from your water bottle—not from the water fountain.
- You must wear a mask during "group time."

These are just a few of the precautions being taken by schools this year to protect children from the deadly virus.

As noted above, drinking from the water fountain is no longer deemed safe; some schools have purchased water bottles for every student. Consider the analogy of students as water bottles: They are valuable because they contain that which is essential to life, and by the time they get to your classroom, they may have been covered with many different labels, shaken vigorously by life, tossed back and forth between caretakers, and left by themselves for too many hours.

Some of our little "water bottles" have suffered a lot of trauma. At least half of them have lived through a divorce, an experience that threatens to split them wide open. Others have been the victims of abuses (directly or indirectly) no person should ever have to endure. Perhaps they have seen a loved one's life threatened by violence or been placed in a position of caring for younger siblings because their parent is incapacitated by drugs. These are situations children should never experience.

(A public school teacher shared with me the following story: She was called to the playground when one of her second-grade students skinned his knee. After contacting his parent and securing permission to apply some ointment and a Band-Aid, she told the child, "When you get home, your mom may want to take you to the drugstore and get some medicine to put on your knee." The student looked at her quizzically, before replying, "You don't get drugs from a store." He had seen drugs purchased before, and in his world, those transactions had never involved a retail establishment.)

Regardless of their exterior conditions, each of these "little bottles" contains a sacred gift—their child-spirit. It was placed inside of them by your Higher Power when they entered this world, and it cannot be contaminated. The Farce has done everything possible to cover up the exterior of the container so that no one can see what is inside, but nothing is hidden from your Higher Power. The child does not know the source of their spirit of love; nor are they aware of the other gifts that lie within themselves.

Unfortunately, you as their teacher or guide cannot access this child-spirit. No matter how much you love the little "water bottles," the inner spirit of the child is only available to your Higher Power, the one who placed it there; it is too holy, to precious, too irreplaceable, to allow humans to interact with it. The water within each student is capable of a great deal, because each tiny drop of this water contains immense power. That power can be a positive explosion that releases a person from whatever has held them back; it can also be a small but persistent driving force that takes years to overcome the obstacles that have blocked it from moving forward.

What you can do for your class of "water bottles" is reflect your Higher Power to them. If they see your Higher Power in your daily interactions with them and their fellow students, their child-spirit will be awakened. Once awakened, the child-spirit is drawn to the Higher Power within you and intuitively seeks to be united with the Love that you represent. The results are miraculous. Imagine your inner Light as a direct reflection of His, shining with an intense brightness in your classroom. Now imagine that same Light being reflected in a classroom full of 20 little "water bottles," each serving as a mirror of His Love. Your classroom can be a place of healing.

What teacher would not want this for their students? Some of you have already begun praying for it to happen in your classroom. Good for you. Lest you get too far into your plans to "make it happen," I will remind you that your task is to empty yourself of yourself each day so that your Higher Power can guide you to do His will. In other words, this is not something you can achieve; it is not something that you can be proud of. This classroom of healing begins with a teacher who is honest, open-minded, and willing to surrender to their Higher Power. To reflect Him, they must also give their character defects to Him, both personal and social. They communicate with Him often, have an intimate relationship with Him, and trust Him completely.

It sounds impossible; it is too idealistic and impractical, says the Farce. That would be true, except for one inescapable truth: If we do the possible, He can and will do the impossible.

An Awesome Day

My vision for teachers is one that they probably will not recognize until after it has occurred. It is my sincere hope and prayer that one day in the not-too-distant future, you will be reviewing the events of the day and slowly begin to realize that it was an awesome one. Not only were the students fairly well-behaved, but they were focused on their work, transitioned well from one activity to the other, and were surprisingly gracious toward you and their classmates. You remember hearing a lot of laughter from them.

This awesome day will require further inspection. Why today? As you allow yourself to reflect further, you start at the beginning of the day. You recall that you were not rushed before work, a rare occurrence indeed. You had time to meditate and spiritually empty yourself of all expectations for the day, and you remember asking just to follow Him today and for help in keeping that prayer within your awareness.

Come to think of it, there were a couple of unusual coincidences that occurred. These happened at just the right time. There is no way to explain the timing, except to acknowledge that your Higher Power was involved. You suddenly feel grateful and happy. As you dwell in these feelings for a few moments, this thought comes to mind: "You are teaching with a Higher Power!" You are not being ungrateful when you ask Him the question that comes next: "Can we do it again tomorrow?"

In *The Absorbent Mind*, Maria Montessori concluded the chapter entitled "The Montessori Teacher" with these words:

> It is not a prayer, but a memorandum, and so for Montessori teachers, an invocation, a kind of syllabus, our only syllabus:
> "HELP US O LORD TO PENETRATE
> INTO THE SECRET OF THE CHILD
> SO THAT WE MAY KNOW HIM,
> LOVE HIM AND SERVE HIM
> ACCORDING TO YOUR LAWS OF
> JUSTICE AND FOLLOWING YOUR
> DIVINE WILL."

BIBLIOGRAPHY

Baker, Irene *Nurturing the Inner Life: The Spiritual Preparation of the Teacher*, https://www.montessoriservices.com/ideas-insights/nurturing-the-inner-life-the-spiritual-preparation-of-the-teacher

Baker, John *Celebrate Recovery Updated Leader's Guide*, Zondervan, 2012

Blackaby, Henry, Blackaby, Richard, and King, Claude *Experiencing God*, Lifeway Press, 2007

Carnegie, Dale *How to Stop Worrying and Start Living*, Simon & Shuster, 1984

Gibran, Kahlil, *The Prophet,* New York: Knopf, 1995

The Holy Bible New International Version, International Bible Society, Zondervan, 1986

Lewis, C.S. *A Mind Awake: An Anthology of C. S. Lewis,* Houghton Mifflin Harcourt, 2003

Lewis, C.S. *Essay on Forgiveness*, Macmillan Publishing Company, 1960

Martin, Joseph *Steps 1-3 of Alcoholics Anonymous*, DVD

McLeod, S. A. (2018, Dec 28). Solomon Asch — Conformity Experiment, https://www.simplypsychology.org/asch-conformity.html

Montessori, Maria *The Absorbent Mind*, BN Publishing, 2012

Montessori, Maria *The Secret of Childhood*, Random House Publishing Group, 1966_

Montessori Print Shop Blog *Normalization: Part One — Discipline*, http://tothelesson.blogspot.com/2011/08/normalization-part-one.html

The North American Montessori Center, *Understanding Normalization and the Montessori Classroom*, Montessori Teacher Training Blog, April 8, 2008

The Twelve Steps for Everyone Who Really Wants Them, Revised Edition, Hazelden, 1990

Twelve Steps and Twelve Traditions, Alcoholics Anonymous World Services Inc., 1987

Warren, Rick *The Purpose-Driven Life*, Zondervan, 2002

Wiles, Mike and Tribble, Byron *The Purple Gorilla in the Classroom*, Think Different Productions, 2004

Wolfelt, Alan _Companioning the Bereaved_, Companion Press, 2006

www.ingramcontent.com/pod-product-compliance
Lightning Source LLC
LaVergne TN
LVHW041545070426
835507LV00011B/940